CATCHING FISH

by
Chet Meyers
and
Al Lindner

DILLON PRESS, INC.   MINNEAPOLIS

© 1978 by Dillon Press, Inc. All rights reserved
Third printing 1980

Dillon Press, Inc., 500 South Third Street
Minneapolis, Minnesota 55415

Printed in the United States of America

Library of Congress Cataloging in Publication Data

Meyers, Chet, 1942-
  Catching fish.
  Includes index.
  1. Fishing. II. Lindner, Al, 1944-   joint author.
II. Title.
SH441.M49   799.1'2   78-6532
ISBN 0-87518-165-1

Contents

To our fathers, Pops and Chet, Senior,
who started us off

Many people help to create a book, and we would like to thank just a few of the many who have helped us: Ron Lindner, the entire staff of *In' Fisherman* magazine, Dan Gapen, Mike Finck, Carl Brookins, Jean Engelmann, Lillian Sundblad, Ron Hagberg, Miriam Meyers, and Jeff Zernov, for his excellent photographs.

Introduction

Hundreds of books have been written about the art of fishing since Izaak Walton penned the first edition of the *Compleat Angler* in 1653. But it was not until very recently that serious studies of fish and fishing have been published. Today there are a number of books available on the biological aspects of game fish and on the structural aspects of fish habitat. Countless more books have provided detailed information on different types of fishing tackle. In what follows we have intentionally stayed away from these topics. This book focuses on a subject far more interesting than the fish or its habitat and far less understood—the fisherman.

Most of us have studied something of the creature that we pursue. We know that fish are creatures of instinct and habit. The problem is that fishermen, too, are creatures of habit. We also develop patterns of behavior, and most of us are painfully aware of how seldom our patterns coincide with the fish's pattern.

At least once or twice during a fishing class that we are teaching, someone will approach one of us at the end of the session and say, "Look! You know all that stuff you've been talking about—structure and seasonal movement and all that? Well, I know all about it. I've read everything that has been written on fishing. I have the best equipment you can buy. And I still don't catch fish. What's wrong?"

After a little more conversation, we can usually discover what's wrong. And most of the time it boils down to one thing—a gap between what the person knows and what he or she can actually do in the boat. There are a lot of "theoretical" anglers. Owning the best equipment and reading the best books will not improve anyone's fishing unless that person knows how to use that equipment and knowledge. We are more and more convinced that most anglers need to forget some of their unproductive fishing habits and learn a variety of new approaches.

In the final analysis, being a successful fisherman means being versatile, and versatility is what this book is all about. It is designed to help anglers learn fishing tactics that will help them cope with any fishing circumstance. It is written for all of us, men and women, who pursue fish not only for the pure joy of relaxing in the outdoors, but also in hopes that someday we will catch the lunker of a lifetime.

chapter 1

The Lost Connection

Modern technological society has brought with it many blessings. One of the sadder aspects of modern life, however, is that most of us have lost the closeness to nature that our parents and grandparents enjoyed. We live and work in artificial environments where we need not be bothered by rain, sleet, cold winds, or blistering heat. In fact, it is not until we get out in a boat or wade in our favorite stream that we are reminded of how harsh nature can be at times. We often tend to view changes in the weather as inconveniences and fail to realize that daily and seasonal cycles of weather have a profound effect on fishing. One crisp fall day on Gull Lake, Al and Ron Lindner made a mistake that many of us make time and time again—they forgot about the rhythm of the natural world.

"When Ron and I hit Gull Lake that morning, we had just returned home from a bass fishing tournament in Texas. We had been on the road for over a week, and the fishing conditions during the tournament were less than ideal. Somehow fishing for walleyes on one of our favorite lakes seemed the best way to unwind after struggling under a broiling sun to haul largemouths out of flooded timber.

"We headed for a little-known gravel bar that had been producing walleyes for us all summer long. I could almost taste those tender batter-fried fillets. Ron cut the motor, and we drifted quietly to the edge of the bar and began casting a jig and minnow combination. After fifteen minutes without a strike, we changed to live bait on a slip sinker and began trolling slowly back and forth along the drop-off and into deep water. We picked up one small perch and decided to move to a sunken island nearby that almost always holds a school of two- or three-pound walleyes. Once again we struck out.

"It wasn't until we were on our way to our next fishing hole that our minds finally began to work. Suddenly, Ron cut the motor and stared at me.

" 'We must have left our brains in Texas,' he said. 'It's the first week in September and—'

" 'And while we were in Texas,' I broke in, 'Minnesota had its first hard frost.'

"Both of us knew what that meant. Those first cold nights had signaled the end of summer, and the walleyes had abandoned their summer hangouts. It wasn't until we readjusted our fishing strategy that we saw our first walleye and that walleye dinner I had been dreaming about became a possibility."

SEASONAL MOVEMENTS OF FISH

As creatures captive to their environment, fish are closely attuned to changes in weather and water conditions, and they respond to these changes by moving around in lakes and rivers. The concept of fish movement is really very simple and not too different from a more dramatic example of instinctive behavior—the annual migration pattern of Canada geese. In the spring of the year, great flocks of Canada geese migrate north from Texas and other southern wintering grounds. They are on their way to northern Canada and Alaska where they will set up spring housekeeping and hatch their young. After breeding they move into regular summer patterns of feeding and raising their families. In the fall, when the first cold winds blow down from the Arctic, they begin preparing for their long flight back to Texas and the southern states.

Fish go through similar seasonal cycles, although their movement is usually confined to the lakes or rivers in which they were hatched. In the spring of the year most game fish migrate into shallow water areas to spawn. This migration is triggered by water temperature, and each species responds to a different temperature. Each species also prefers a different set of bottom conditions to spawn over. Walleyes, for example, like hard gravel bottoms while northern pike prefer shallow, weedy sloughs. After the spawn, fish begin to move into a summer location pattern, usually choosing another area of the lake. This movement also is triggered by water temperature and is in response to locating prey that the game fish will feed on all summer long. Once this pattern is established, fish location will be fairly predictable throughout the summer. With the arrival of the first cold nights that precede the fall, lakes and rivers cool off rather quickly, and once again the fish move to a new location. In the North, where lakes ice over, ice fishermen usually find a gradual movement of game fish from shallow to deeper water as the winter progresses. In the South, fish also move deeper and become less active, but daily weather conditions can make dramatic changes if a warm spell sends the water temperature soaring. As spring approaches, fish begin to move back to their spawning grounds, and the cycle is complete.

Although there are many subtle changes in weather and water conditions, we can simplify things if we think in terms of the four major seasonal cycles. Since these cycles are a function of water temperature and the movement of prey,

This small bay may be teeming with spawning northerns in late April and totally devoid of fish by the end of May.

they do not necessarily follow the days on our calendar. An early spring or a late fall can make all the difference in where the fish will be. For them, patterns of movement are simply an instinctual response to water temperature, sexual needs, and the pursuit of prey.

- *The spring pattern:* This includes a short period prior to spawning when the fish are moving into their spawning ground, the actual spawn, and a short time after spawning is completed. Each species spawns at a different water temperature and seeks its preferred bottom conditions. There will be some regional differences in spawning temperature. For example, walleyes in northern Manitoba spawn at a colder temperature than do Kentucky walleyes. The best areas to fish are those in and around the actual spawning grounds, especially where there is deep water nearby.

- *The summer pattern:* In many parts of the country a good indication that fish may have established their summer pattern is that the water is warm enough for a pleasant swim. Depending on your region the summer pattern may last anywhere from three to five months. In summer, game fish are located primarily in relation to prey that they feed upon regularly. Typical summer hot spots include sunken islands, shallow bars that run into deep water, and newly emerging weed beds.

- *The fall pattern:* This usually begins after the first hard frost, when the cold nights set in at the end of summer. The water temperature falls to the fifty-five-degree range, and you won't want to go swimming for long. This cold water period signals another change in the location of game fish and prey. Typically, we see briefer periods of feeding and frequent movements into shallow water. The best fishing spots can be the sharper drop-offs near shallow water feeding grounds.

- *The winter pattern:* The behavior of fish in winter varies greatly according to geographical location. Some areas of the South experience little freezing weather, while northern lakes may have up to three feet of ice on them. The colder the water temperature, the less active the fish and the less often they will be feeding. Different species behave differently. In the North when there is ice on the lakes, largemouth and smallmouth bass become almost dormant, while walleyes, though less active than during the fall, feed all winter long. Fish movement is difficult to predict, but winter anglers agree that because fish are less active, the slower you can present your lure or bait, the better.

Once we discover a seasonal location, we know that the fish are usually in the general vicinity. When the seasons change, however, game fish movement is almost inevitable. Let's go back to that day on Gull Lake for an example of how these seasonal patterns work. Ron and Al knew they had established a summer pattern off the gravel bar and near the sunken island. But after sweltering under the heat of a Texas sky and fishing for bass, they forgot about weather conditions in Minnesota. When an early hard frost hit and a series of cold nights followed, it was a sure prelude to a new location for walleyes. Cold nights cause the top layer of water to cool off rapidly. As this layer of water cools, it becomes heavy and begins to sink to the bottom, creating a very slight current that forces lower layers of water toward the surface. We call this "fall turnover" because the water in the lake actually does turn over. This general mixing of a lake's water temporarily disorients the fish, and they abandon their summer hideouts. Fall turnover happens very quickly. If you fish your favorite lake only on weekends, you may not be aware that it has taken place. It doesn't take long, however, to figure out that something has changed because you just won't catch many fish in your summer hot spots, and if you decide to take a swim, you will probably exit twice as fast as you entered.

The best way to respond to any seasonal movement of game fish is to cover a lot of water. Try trolling slowly or drift fishing, but keep moving. During the transition between any of the patterns we have outlined, the fish are regrouping in another location. The move will not be immediate, but once a new seasonal pattern is established, the fish will stay in that general area. If you know your lake well, these patterns become fairly predictable year after year. Northern pike and bass patterns of movement are usually very easy to predict. Walleyes roam around a little more, but even they can be "psyched-out" with a little time and effort.

LEARNING THE SEASONAL PATTERNS ON YOUR LAKE OR RIVER

With the aid of a log book, a thermometer, and a hydrographic map (depth map), you can establish the seasonal patterns for game fish on your body of water. It is necessary to make enough trips to your lake or river so that you can really identify different location patterns, but the results will be well worth the time. Once you learn the seasonal patterns on your body of water, not only will you catch more fish, but you will also be able to discover the seasonal patterns on other lakes and rivers much more easily.

In chapter 5 we have some hints for selecting a good fishing lake, but now let's assume that you know of a lake that has a healthy population of the game fish you are after. Just be sure that you don't use convenience as your only reason for selecting a body of water. We know of one man who spent four years fishing a nearby lake for big walleyes that "just had to be there." Not only did the lake have no big walleyes, it had darn few walleyes of any size! Check with your state department of natural resources, and make sure the fish are there before you go after them.

First, get a hydrographic map that shows the bottom contour of the lake. Most departments of natural resources have these maps or can tell you where to get one. Don't expect the map to be perfect. Hydrographic maps often miss some of the hot spots on a lake. Make reduced copies of the map and take one with you on every trip and mark each fish you catch according to its location. Try to identify the spawning places, summer locations, and cold water locations.

After working on your lake for a while, your hydrographic map might look something like the one shown on page 15.

A daily log will help you record such information as the location of the fish you catch, cloud cover, general weather conditions, and water temperature. Start keeping such a log and record every trip to your lake. Buy an inexpensive thermometer so that you can keep track of the spring spawning temperatures and the time of the fall turnover. During most of the summer, temperature is not that big a factor.

On page 16 is the format of a simplified log that may be modified to meet your own particular needs. Type one master and then reproduce enough copies to last the whole fishing season. A pocket notebook is handy for keeping the sheets together.

It is crucial to keep a log of your trips because you just cannot remember all the specifics of weather and water conditions. You might not have difficulty remembering some of the hot spots where you caught fish, but you will not remember the water temperature or weather conditions.

The most important thing to remember about seasonal patterns is that they occur not by our calendar, but by the calendar of the fish. And the fish's calendar is pretty much a function of water temperature. With the exception of a few species of trout, most game fish spawning in North America occurs in the spring of the year but not until the water temperature is just right. By studying your particular species and finding the type of bottom it prefers, by talking with other anglers, and by doing some scouting around

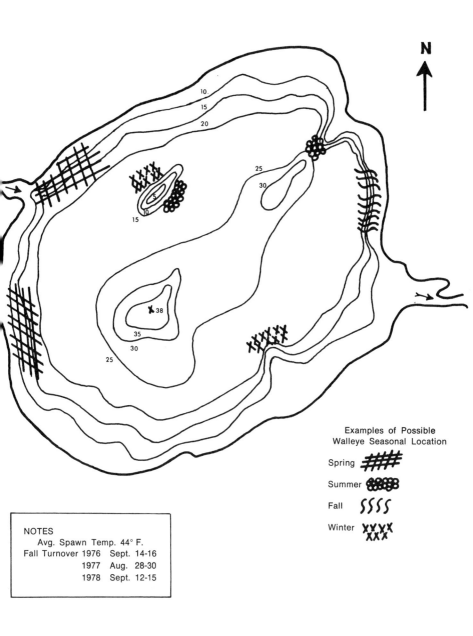

N

Examples of Possible
Walleye Seasonal Location

Spring ####

Summer 🌑🌑🌑🌑

Fall ſſſſ

Winter XXXX
XXX

NOTES
Avg. Spawn Temp. 44° F.
Fall Turnover 1976   Sept. 14-16
           1977   Aug. 28-30
           1978   Sept. 12-15

Using a hydrographic map to record seasonal movements of fish.

A typical log sheet.

your lake, you should be able to locate some of the spawning areas. Since many lakes are now stocked, you will want to contact your department of natural resources to see if natural spawning does occur in your lake. If it does not, the location of spawning grounds will not be important, but the fish will still establish a spring locational pattern. If your lake does have a natural spawning population and you know some of the spawning areas, try to find others. In most lakes, usually only the largest and best-known spawning areas are fished.

After the spawning season, try to establish where in the lake the fish move for their summer pattern. Depending on weather conditions, this may take a few weeks. Recording water temperature in your log for each trip will help you determine when the summer pattern is finally established.

During the summer pattern, water temperature is not that big a factor, but in the fall you will want to be aware of sudden changes in water temperature that signal fall turnover. Once the "cold water" fishing period begins, the fish will remain in it until freezeup.

While it might take a while to locate these seasonal fishing areas, it is the key to understanding your lake. There is no magic involved. It just takes time, a little record-keeping, and an appreciation of the natural world and its seasonal cycles.

DAILY MOVEMENTS OF FISH

Once you have established that fish move around in a lake or river for a reason, you are on your way to more fish on the stringer and fewer alibis. You can begin to predict where they will be at any given time of the year, and it is only a matter of refinement to understand how daily weather conditions will determine where they will be found on any given day.

Let's say that you have discovered a sunken gravel island where the walleyes usually hang out during the summer. They will be in this general vicinity most of the summer, but that doesn't mean you are going to catch your limit every time out. On bright sunny days the walleyes may drop down into deeper water off either end of the island. On cloudy days they may move up on top. If the sunken island is a shallow one, then wind velocity and direction will play an important role in determining how the fish relate to the island. If you think the fish are in this general area, then try different depths and different lures or baits. And be sure to move all over that piece of water!

A log of your fishing trips becomes really important in understanding these daily fish movements. If you keep a log, pretty soon you will be able to predict how the fish will react to sun and wind and rain. Some patterns will be fairly predictable and will make sense. Others you will just stumble on, and they will amaze you, as Chet Meyers discovered last year.

"My friend Ron Hagberg and I were fishing a small-mouth bass lake in southern Manitoba, and for the first few days we were catching bass regularly in eight to ten feet of water. The weather was sunny, and there was a slight wind with a little chop on the water. The third day of our trip, the sun was shining as usual, but it was dead calm. We knew that we had discovered a summer pattern and that the bass would not be far from where we had caught them the day before, but we predicted that with the calm they would be in deeper water. We started out in ten feet of water and began working deeper with leeches and nightcrawlers. When live bait failed to pay off, we went to deep-running lures and continued to work deeper. Soon we were in thirty feet of water, the deepest part of the lake in that area, and hadn't seen a fish. Where had they gone? Had they abandoned the area, or were they just not hitting? After a couple of hours and no fish, we put our rods down and started thinking.

"Lots of things seemed logical, but nothing was paying off. For two days we had identified a pattern that the lack of wind had broken. It seemed logical to think that the fish had moved deeper, but we had not picked up a fish all morning in deep water. We were up against a stone wall. Finally, I turned to Ron and suggested something rather absurd.

" 'Listen, why not move in shallower and see if the bass are close to shore?'

"Ron was skeptical, but he turned the boat around and headed toward shore. We started at about ten feet and followed the gradually sloping bottom up. We could see our lures in the crystal clear water, and with a clean bottom except for a few cracks in the granite, it seemed hopeless. I cast my yellow Shyster towards the shore and was watching my retrieve across the bottom. I could see that there were no bass. As the lure passed over one of the cracks in the granite, I felt a snag. Suddenly, a two-pound smallmouth exploded out of the water. My mouth dropped and Ron turned only to say, 'Where the hell did he come from?' The bass were hiding in the cracks between the huge granite slabs that formed the lake bottom. In the next half hour we took six good-sized bass out of water that was one to three feet deep. Then I pushed our experiment to its logical conclusion.

" 'Let's move in closer.'

"Ron nodded, and I changed to a small floating Rapala to prevent getting hung up. I dropped the Rapala between two small rocks in six inches of water. The fish must have been lying on its side, for a ten-inch smallie came rocketing out of the water! I know it doesn't make sense, but for over an hour we worked a pattern that really produced. When a slight wind put a ripple on top of the water, the bass stopped hitting. Maybe these were backward bass, and they had moved out into deeper water. We are still not sure why it happened, but having put six nice bass on the stringer, we weren't about to complain."

Daily patterns seldom last for long periods of time. Often the slightest change in weather conditions will disrupt a pattern. The wind that came up while Ron and Chet were catching those bass was not a strong wind, but it was enough to move the bass out of the shallows. We have seen schools of fish begin feeding when a few puffy clouds briefly obscured the sun and then cease feeding when the sun shone brightly. A change in the direction of the wind can move a school of walleyes or bass from one end of a sunken island to the other end. River fish are very sensitive to fluctuations in water level and change their location and

Smallmouth like this can be taken in very shallow water if the seasonal and daily patterns are right.

feeding behavior accordingly. If the weather remains stable for three or four days with no perceptible changes in air temperature, wind speed and direction, and amount of sunlight, the location and feeding time of the fish is fairly predictable. On other occasions when there are two or three weather changes in a single day, the fish move around a lot.

MAKING THE CONNECTION

There are really only two ways to fish. You can sit and wait for the fish to come to you, or you can go after them. Now there is nothing wrong with sitting all day with rod in hand and waiting them out. It is very relaxing, and sometimes that's just what you need. But if you are interested not only in fishing, but also in catching fish, you have a better chance of success if you seek them out. If you have a favorite fishing hole, remember it is probably a seasonal location. If it doesn't produce, try moving around. It's a good idea to spend no more than fifteen minutes in any one place without catching fish.

Once you get back in touch with the natural world, fish movement will become less of a mystery. If you are alert to seasonal and daily changes in weather conditions and if you keep a record of fish-catching locations, patterns will begin to emerge. After a while, your movements will start matching those of the fish, and that can only mean better fishing.

chapter 2

Fishing Where the Fish Are

Chet Meyers has always had a special fondness for rivers ever since he spent his first days of fishing on the beautiful streams and rivers of western Pennsylvania. He has this story to tell about his baffling introduction to river fishing in Minnesota.

"When I knew I was moving to Minnesota, rivers were on my mind, and not long after my arrival, I came across the name of one of the few active fishing guides on the Saint Croix River. The guide, whom I'll call Harry, was seventy-eight years old and a river fisherman from way back. When I called his home, his wife informed me that Harry was out on the river at the moment but that he did have an opening for the following Saturday. She gave me directions to their home and told me what equipment to bring—a nine-foot fly rod and half a dozen yellow and white bass bugs. I spent the next six evenings in my backyard, frantically trying to figure out how to work a fly rod and entertaining half the neighborhood with my antics. By the time Saturday morning arrived, I was less than confident, so I brought along my ultralight spinning rod, just in case.

"The day was beautiful, the scenery was breathtaking, and Harry was very patient. After the first hour, he leaned forward and said, 'You're going to have to pick up that line quicker—you've missed five bass so far.' Well, the nine-foot fly rod and I just didn't make a pair. After a second hour of frustration, I laid the monster down and began assembling my ultralight spinning rod. I could tell that Harry was skeptical, but he just turned around and continued rowing down the river. We would drift down the river, and Harry would tell me where to cast. His accuracy in predicting where the bass would be was amazing. It seemed that he knew every bass in the river by name. Every so often Harry would ask me to reel in, and he would row us to the other side of the river. In the four hours before lunch, we must have crossed the river five or six times. By that time we had a few nice bass in the ice chest, and I was beginning to understand what Harry was doing.

"Harry had identified a summer pattern for smallmouth bass, and that pattern consisted of fishing rock piles. The lower section of the Saint Croix is a very sandy stretch of river, but every so often there are limestone outcroppings that run along the shore. Since smallmouth bass feed primarily on crayfish and other crustacea, and since crayfish live in rock piles, Harry just kept his eye peeled for the limestone rock piles and fished them. Every time we crossed the river, it was to avoid a sandy stretch and to pick up a rock pile. Harry had lived on the river for sixty years, and he knew its shoreline like the back of his hand. His identification of this pattern paid off for his customers in regular limits of bass. But for all his years and wisdom, Harry had a problem—he was stubborn.

"After lunch we were crossing the river to reach one of his rock piles when I noticed a partially submerged reef in the middle of the river. I asked Harry to hold the boat so I could make a few casts. To my surprise, he refused. 'There aren't any bass in the *middle* of the river' was all he said as we continued to drift downstream. Well, as much as I respected his years of experience, I couldn't resist turning and making a fleeting cast at the reef. After one turn of the handle the rod bucked in my hands. 'See! Now you've gone and got hung up,' he snorted. I told him that I had a bass on, but he just grunted and began rowing the boat back to where I was 'hung up.' Suddenly, the bass exploded out of the water in front of the boat. Harry had his pride— he just turned around and began to row back down the river. He refused to net the bass, and to this day I don't think he ever acknowledged the fact that I caught a bass in the middle of the river."

FISHING THE SHORELINE

Harry was in a rut. He was fishing the shoreline for visible objects and completely avoiding the rest of the river. This is natural behavior. We all like to see where we are fishing, and since most of us have difficulty envisioning what the bottom of a lake or river looks like, we usually end up casting towards things we can see. We are all confirmed shoreline fishermen. Put most of us on a large body of water, particularly a new lake that we have never fished before, and very soon we start feeling overwhelmed by all that water. Our response is usually quick and predictable. We head for the shoreline and spend most of our time casting towards those reliable objects that we have been taught "look fishy." We look for lily pads, boat docks, and over-hanging trees. Every once in a while we might venture out towards the middle of the lake, but once again, we fish around an island or a reed bed. The diagram opposite indicates some of the classic objects that anglers seek while fishing the shoreline.

If you ask most shoreline anglers where the fish are located in their lake, you will probably get the kind of pic-

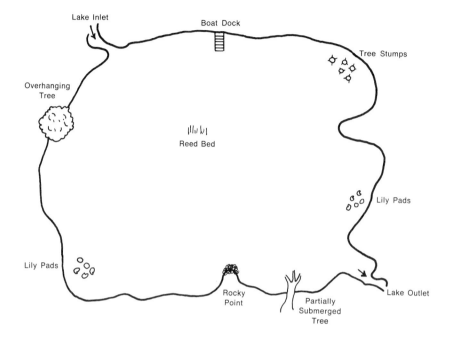

Most of us grew up learning to fish shoreline structure like this.

ture shown in the top diagram on page 26. If each dot equals a fish, you can see that in the mind of the shoreline angler, most of the fish are located close to shore and scattered pretty evenly along the shore, with a few clusters by lily pads and overhanging trees. Is this a true picture? Where are the fish located in most lakes?

STRUCTURE FISHING AND DEEP WATER LOCATIONS

As long as anglers could see only the shoreline, it was natural that they would stick pretty close to it and, of course, we have all caught fish there. It was not until the depth finder was introduced in the late 1950s that anglers

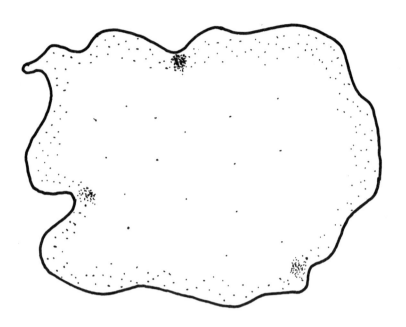

Which is the true picture of where fish will be found?

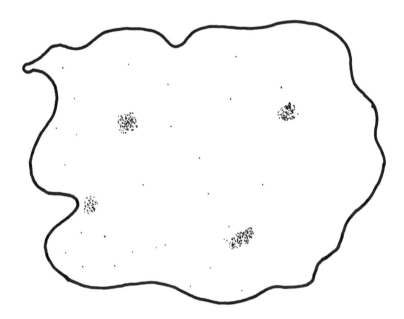

A school of one Hundred walleyes can be very tightly packed.

began to realize that there were fish out in the middle of the lake as well. They began to give attention to the bottom of lakes and rivers. Much of the pioneering in this area was done by Buck Perry, a geologist and avid fisherman. It was Perry who started catching fish in deep water and who believes that deep water is the home of most game fish. According to his theory of fishing, about 90 percent of any lake or river is devoid of fish. Instead, the fish are concentrated in a very small part of the total area of a body of water. This theory seems to be borne out by the observations of skin divers. Fish are by nature schooling creatures, and unless you have been underwater yourself, it is almost impossible to believe how small a space a school of two hundred walleye can occupy. While schooling behavior varies somewhat from one lake to another, it is safe to assume that fish spend much of their time traveling in schools. Fish operate by instinct, and for them, there is safety in numbers. According to this new theory, which we call structure fishing, fish are actually distributed as shown in the bottom diagram on page 26.

Now that's quite a different picture than we used to have about fish location. Which of the pictures is correct? Well, the second one has much more truth to it than does the one visualized by the shoreline fisherman. This doesn't mean that all the fish are in deep water, but it does mean that if you are fishing only the shoreline, you are missing a lot of nice fish.

The reasoning behind structure fishing is not difficult to understand if we think of the fish as an instinctual animal and investigate its basic survival needs. Three basic drives determine most of a fish's behavior patterns: safety, food, and reproduction. Since it is only during the short spawning season that reproduction takes precedence over the other two, we can ignore this drive except for a few weeks in spring. In its day-to-day existence, the need for safety and food control how and where a fish will move.

From the first day it hatches, a fish is constantly being pursued by something else that wants to eat it. When fish hatch in shallow water, many of their predators come from above the water in the form of herons, kingfishers, and other birds and animals that feed in the shallows. Thus, very early in their lives, fish view deep water as a refuge. Even when they grow big enough to be the predator and not the prey, their early memories remain with them. While deep water means safety, however, most of the food in most lakes is located on shallow water food shelves. How does a fish satisfy these two contradictory needs?

The answer is really simple if you accept structure theory. It assumes that fish spend most of their time in deep water and that they make regular movements to shallow water food shelves, grab a quick meal, and move back to deep water. To do this, fish travel along regular routes. Usually the quickest path from deep water to food is the best. The word "structure" refers to those elements of a lake or river that are different from the surrounding area and that help fish orient themselves to the location of both food and safety. A rock reef protruding from a flat bottom is structure; so are drop-offs, or noticeable "breaks" from shallow to deep water. Weed beds and many of our shoreline favorites are also referred to as structure.

Structure exists anytime there is a noticeable break with the surrounding area. The key to successful fishing, according to structure theory, is to locate those areas where there is an easy connection between deep water and a supply of food and where structure is present.

As structure theory became known, many anglers, armed with hydrographic maps, depth finders, and their new knowledge, left the shoreline and ventured forth seeking those "honey holes" in deep water that held the big fish. Instead of docks and overhanging trees, they began to look for new objects to fish, like sharp drop-offs and shallow bars that ran out into deep water, The hydrographic map on page 30 indicates some of the classic structure that this new breed of angler sought.

THE PROBLEM WITH FISHING STRUCTURE

Structure fishing, depth finders, and hydrographic maps helped many of us break the habit of fishing only the shoreline, but for some it merely replaced one unthinking routine with another. What such anglers fail to realize is that the location of structure, whether it be lily pads or a sunken island, does not by itself guarantee successful fishing. Something that happened to Chet Meyers about four years ago should bring this point home.

"It was not long after my friends and I started reading about structure and depth finders that I discovered what I

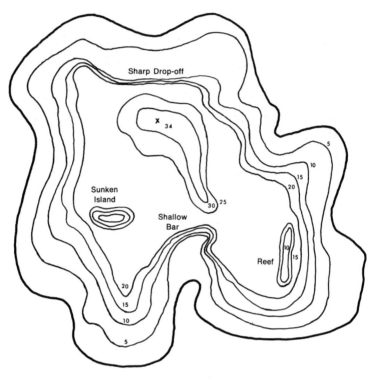

This is the type of structure that today's angler looks for.

thought was a lunker hole on my favorite river. I was drifting down the Saint Croix one afternoon, when suddenly the orange flasher on my depth finder jumped from three feet to twenty-five. Since I was late getting home, I made a few casts, caught a small bass, and mentally marked the spot for a future trip. I was so excited that I couldn't keep the secret, so I called a fishing friend and promised him a trip to my new lunker hole. Two weeks later we got away for the trip. We worked the hole over for a couple of hours. Although we caught only a couple of small bass, I just knew the big ones were down there.

"I returned to that hole a number of times, once collecting a three-pound walleye, but no lunkers. Still I went back, convinced that they were there, and I just had to wait them out. Luckily, a fishing log I keep on each trip brought me to my senses. One cold December evening, I was sitting by the fire, reviewing last year's log, when I realized that I had made eight trips, spent over twenty hours, and caught only six fish from that hole. As a friend said to me later, 'You may have found some beautiful structure, but what good is structure without fish?' "

The temptation to fish shoreline structure or deep water structure is very strong. And while the statement that fish usually relate to some type of structure is a valid generalization, it is risky to assume that just because you have found structure, you will find fish.

The point of this chapter is not to discourage either shoreline or deep water fishing. Both will produce fish. Just don't get hung up on fishing structure because it looks as if it has to hold fish. Some lily pads will consistently produce bass, while other lily pads fifty yards away will not. Some gravel reefs hold large schools of walleyes while others haven't hosted a walleye in years. There are lakes

Granite reefs like this one are plentiful in the Canadian boundary waters, but not all of them hold fish.

in the boundary waters of Minnesota that would drive a deep water structure fisherman crazy—there are rock reefs, sharp drop-offs, and gravel bars everywhere, and most of them are devoid of fish. The trick is to learn how to distinguish good fish-holding structure from just plain structure.

FINDING WHERE THE FISH REALLY ARE

While there is no one way to locate good fish-holding structure, we can make a few suggestions that should help you eliminate unproductive water. Remember, the only reason game fish are attracted to an area on a regular basis is that it provides them access to both food and safety.

- *Be aware of the depth at which you catch fish.* We have stated that fish seek out deep water as a refuge. How deep is deep enough? In clear lakes fish may spend most of their time in water over twenty feet deep. In murky lakes the same fish will hold shallower. The reason for this behavior is that light penetration is greater in clear lakes. Fish usually avoid light, since they equate light with vulnerability. When you catch a fish, make a note of the depth at which you hooked it and keep this information in your log book.

- *Analyze the bottom conditions where you catch fish.* Weedbeds on hard mud bottoms, broken rock bottoms, or gravel bottoms produce more game fish than do soft muck or sand bottoms. Try to identify the bottom conditions in your lake or river that consistently produce fish. Lily pads that are close to deep water and to other types of weeds produce better than lily pads in shallow water. Similarly, bars that run from shallow to deep water usually produce better if they are close to weedbeds or if they have broken rock bottoms where crayfish can hide. Once you identify the conditions that

Southern anglers learn to recognize locational patterns in flooded timber. Bass are often found where limbs intersect underwater.

produce, look elsewhere for the same conditions.

- *Don't continue to fish places just because they "look fishy."* Keep a daily log and review your log at the end of the year. How many fish did you actually catch at your favorite spots? If a given area doesn't produce after five or six visits under different conditions, forget about it and look elsewhere.

Just remember Harry's Rule, "There aren't any bass in the *middle* of the river," and don't make any such rules for yourself. If you are a shoreline fisherman, venture forth into the lake and try fishing a sunken island. If you spend most of your time in the middle of the lake, come back to the shoreline and look for some hot spots close in. Analyze where and why you are catching fish. The most successful anglers are those who can visualize the bottom conditions they are fishing and those who are constantly alert for new forms of fish-holding structure.

chapter 3

In Among
the Weeds

Pity the poor water weeds. Resort owners curse them as
they try to keep their swimming areas clear of vegetation.
Pleasure boaters utter profanities as they lift their heavy
motors to tear off the "green menace" that has fouled their
propellers. And, finally, fishermen grumble under their
breath as they clean weeds from their favorite lures. Even
the most frustrated angler will admit, however, that fish
utilize water weeds. Moreover, water weeds can tell us a
number of things about the lake or river that we are fishing.

SIGNPOSTS TO GOOD FISHING

Weeds are a good general indicator of the overall fertility
of a body of water. Fertility has to do with the geological
age of a lake. Young lakes are typified by those that are
found in the granite shield area of Canada. Their bottoms
are strewn with large granite boulders and crushed rock,
and they support very little vegetation. The older a lake
gets, the more the rocks weather and break down. The
weathering process builds up soil on the bottom of the lake
and the more soil there is, the more weeds are present.

Limnologists, scientists who study lakes and their aging process, classify young lakes as infertile and old lakes as fertile. While rocky Canadian lakes with few weeds are at the young end of the spectrum, the muddy, weed-choked lakes of the South are a good example of old, fertile lakes. Weed growth is of interest to anglers because it is a good indicator of where fish locate. In a young lake that has very little weed growth, the few weeds that are there may be a key fish attractor. If only 2 or 3 percent of an entire lake can support healthy weed growth, it makes sense to check out those areas to see if game fish are using the weeds. On the other hand, if a lake can support an abundance of weeds, some weeds will hold fish and others will not. In fertile lakes it is not merely the presence of weeds but the presence of certain types of weeds that is the key to fishing success.

A second important fact that weeds tell us about a lake and its fishing potential is the depth to which sunlight penetrates. Most weeds can grow and flourish only if there is enough sunlight available. Naturally, the clearer the water, the deeper the weed growth. In crystal-clear lakes weeds often grow to a depth of twenty feet or more, while in murky lakes water weeds may cease growing at a depth of four or five feet. Because water clarity in a lake is fairly consistent, once you locate the depth of the weedline (the maximum depth to which weeds will grow), you can follow that level on a depth finder and be fairly sure you are close to the weedline. Since the weedline is often an important fish attractor, knowing its depth can help you locate productive fishing water.

Water weeds also give clues to the composition of the lake bottom on which they grow. Each plant has its own ecological niche and grows only where the right soil and bottom conditions are present. Cattails grow on soft muck bottoms. Reeds generally grow in sandy bottom conditions.

Certain forms of pondweed, or cabbage, need a hard mud bottom in order to grow. Such hints are of interest to anglers because fish prefer different bottom conditions during spawning and at other times of the year.

Northerns like to spawn in soft muck bottom sloughs, which are often surrounded by cattails. Walleyes, on the other hand, prefer a hard gravel bottom with little weed growth. And bass choose a hard mud bottom mixed with sand or gravel—the type of bottom that will support only certain kinds of weeds.

One of the most important reasons that fish lurk in the weeds is that vegetation provides both an excellent food source and protection from other predators. The jungle-like environment of thick weeds supports an amazing number of different life forms. Many insects lay their eggs on vegetation, and during the larva stage some insects live entirely underwater. Weed beds attract plankton, small life forms that feed on plankton, a variety of water insects, and crustacea. This developing food chain in turn attracts minnows and small fish, as well as frogs and crayfish, and provides a real smorgasbord for visiting game fish. Smaller fish come to the weeds to seek food and protection, and the larger fish cruise around, hoping to scare up a quick meal from the smaller fish. While most of us think only of large-mouth bass as a weed-loving game fish, almost every game fish—walleye, northern pike, muskie, smallmouth bass, and trout—will at some time be in and around the weeds.

Besides providing a source of food and protection from predators, weeds also give fish a way to escape the penetrating rays of the sun. Many fish head for deep water when the sun's rays glare through the water, but there is more and more evidence that some fish prefer to hide from the sun in weeds. A recent study on Al Lindner's home lake near Brainerd, Minnesota, has shown that some largemouth bass spend most of their lives in shallow, weedy water that may be only one or two feet deep. There seem to be different personality traits among fish, just as among people, and some bass love the weeds. The sun may be shining brightly overhead, but when buried under an inch or two of floating vegetation, these particular bass couldn't care less.

Finally, there are certain times of the year when fish are attracted to underwater vegetation because of the oxygen it generates. Fish need oxygen dissolved in water to survive. Most of the time there is enough dissolved oxygen produced by the continuous action of wind and waves, but there are occasions, particularly during long periods of hot, windless weather, when the supply becomes depleted, and then water weeds become a crucial source. During hot, calm periods, the oxygen which they create tends to concentrate in and around the weed beds. As other areas of the lake lose oxygen, fish migrate to the weeds in order to survive. This creates circumstances that go against folk wisdom. Walleye fishermen have long believed that during the "dog days" of July and August, the walleyes are in the deepest, coolest part of the lake. The only problem is that, if the weather has been hot and calm, those thirty- and forty-foot depths may be losing their oxygen. Anglers may be fishing in forty feet of water, while the walleyes are in a weedbed where the water may be only eight feet deep. On those days the only people catching walleyes are those who are fishing for bass in the weeds.

HOW TO IDENTIFY WATER WEEDS

Since the presence of weeds has an important bearing on fish behavior, a little basic knowledge of aquatic vegetation can enhance your fishing skills. You don't need to become a specialist. The objective is to be sure that if you catch fish in a certain type of weed bed, you can recognize the weed the next time you see it. Often different weeds help us discover a pattern of location on a lake, and being able to distinguish between curly cabbage and tobacco cabbage can make the difference between a good or bad day of fishing.

One of the best ways to learn to recognize the different weed types is to spend an hour or so in an aquarium store. While there are bound to be a few exotic tropical varieties, most of the weeds you will see grow in local lakes and rivers. You can usually find examples of eel grass, coontail, water milfoil, and cabomba. At first glance they may look pretty much alike, but you will quickly discover that they are very different, and the shape of the leaf is usually the key to this difference.

We often break down weeds into two simple categories: hard bottom and soft bottom. Since most of the time most fish prefer a hard bottom habitat, we will focus our attention on this type of vegetation. The following classification should provide most of the basics you need to identify the different weed types.

Soft Bottom Weeds

- *Cattails (Typhaceae):* Found in marshy areas, cattails are usually identified with waterfowl habitat. They grow in a muck-type bottom and are seldom a good indicator of fish habitat except in early spring when northern pike will use these weedy areas for spawning. Largemouth bass may sometimes use floating mats of cattails for cover.

- *Lily pads (Nymphaeaceae):* While some lilies and lotus grow on hard bottoms, most grow in soft muck. They are easily recognized by their large floating leaves and flowering blooms. Lilies can hold largemouth bass when combined with other weed growth or easy access to deep water.

Reeds can grow on hard or soft sand bottoms.

Cattails are one indication of a muck bottom.

Hard Bottom Weeds

- *Reeds or bulrushes (Scirpus):* There are different types. Some grow on soft sand bottoms, and others prefer hard sand bottoms. Most are identified by their spikelike stalks that protrude above the surface of the water. Reeds grow in shallow water, and when the bottom is hard, they can be a good indicator of a largemouth bass spawning area. Some largemouth may use the reeds throughout the year if they provide a source of food and access to cover or deep water.

- *Sand grass (Chara and Nitella):* Sand grass is not really a weed, but a form of algae. This plant is completely submerged. In northern states it can be a prime indicator of largemouth spawning habitat. Sand grass is a

Most lily pads grow on muck or mud bottoms.

ragged, matted algae that seldom grows more than a foot off the bottom and gives off a musky odor when crushed between the fingers.

- *Eel grass (Vallisneria):* This weed grows completely submerged on a hard mud bottom or on mud mixed with sand and gravel. It has long, single-bladed leaves and is an excellent producer of oxygen. Eel grass will attract walleyes and northerns during hot, calm weather.

- *Cabomba (Cabomba):* A weed with tiny feathery leaves, cabomba grows submerged on hard mud bottoms. Clumps of this weed grow up and form an umbrella shape that fish like to hide under. Cabomba is a difficult weed to fish properly because of fish location and because the weed clings to hooks.

- *Coontail or hornwort (Ceratophyllacaeae):* Another feathery weed, whose stalks resemble a raccoon's tail, coontail grows on hard mud bottoms in very thick clumps. This weed often grows up like a Christmas tree, and fish will suspend over it. It is a difficult weed to fish because it, too, clings to hooks. Coontail can, however, be an excellent fish producer when lures and baits are fished just over the tops of the clumps.

- *Cabbage (Potamogetonaceae):* One of the best all-round fish producers, cabbage will attract every species of game fish. It grows on a variety of bottoms from semihard to very hard. There are over three dozen varieties in the continental United States. Cabbage grows submerged except for small flowering tips, which extend an inch or two above the surface. A few varieties have floating leaves. Although it looks forbidding, this is an easy weed to fish in because it is brittle, and lures usually tear free with a quick snap.

Cabomba
(*Cabomba caroliniana* Gray)

Coontail
(*Ceratophyllum demersum* L.)

Sand Grass
(*Nitella Species, Chara species*)

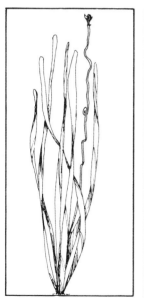

Eel Grass
(*Vallisneria americana* Michx.)

Tobacco Cabbage
(*Potamogeton Amplifolius*)

Curly Cabbage
(*Potamogeton Crispus* L.)

Underwater weeds.

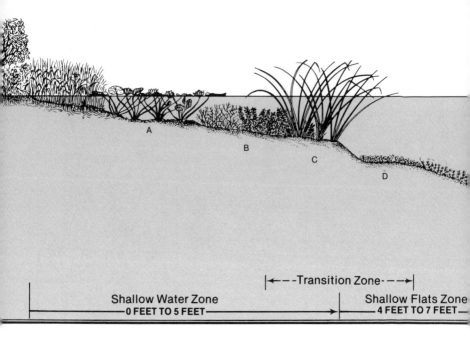

Growth zones of weeds: (a) lily pads, (b) junk weeds, (c) reeds,

WHAT TO LOOK FOR IN THE WEEDS

Weeds should be treated like any other type of structure and should not be fished randomly. Don't just locate a weed bed and start casting, since fish concentrate in certain areas of the bed and avoid others. An experience Chet Meyers and one of his fishing buddies, Cecil Underwood, had one cool August afternoon bears this out.

Since the sun was shining brightly and the water was a flat calm, Chet and Cecil weren't expecting to do very well. They had just decided that their poor luck was the result of a cold front and were bemoaning their fate when a two-pound largemouth pounced on Chet's crank bait. On the next cast, Cecil had a bass of the same size. In seven casts they landed five bass, all in the two-pound category.

The fish were located in an area the size of a bathtub. The weed bed had an almost perfectly square shape, and

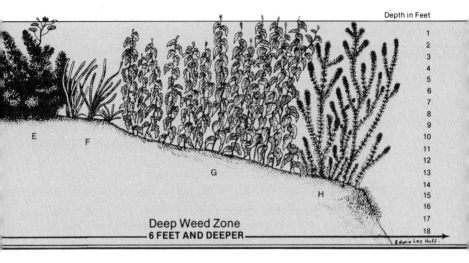

Depth in Feet
1
2
3
4
5
6
7
8
9
10
11
12
13
14
15
16
17
18

E

F

G

H

Deep Weed Zone
6 FEET AND DEEPER

Edwin Lee Huff.

(d) sand grass, (e) cabomba, (f) vallisneria, (g) cabbage, (h) coontail.

©In' Fisherman magazine

all of their bass came from one of the corners where the weeds ceased growing and deep water began. The action died as quickly as it had started. They sought out similar weed beds close to deep water, but none of them produced. After four fruitless hours of fishing, they headed in but, naturally, made one last pass at their "honey hole." Amazingly, the bass were back, and on six casts they landed four more bass, the same size as the ones they had caught in the same spot four hours earlier. Once again the fish were located in an incredibly small area. If a cast was two or three feet from the exact corner of the weed bed, the fish ignored it completely. Had they not known the location of that weed bed and particularly the corner where the weeds broke into deep water, they probably would have been skunked. But the fish were there, and a little knowledge of weeds really paid off.

Here are some general pointers that may help you put your knowledge of weeds to work:

- Try to locate the outside edge of the weedline and determine how deep the weeds grow on your particular lake. If the water clarity is constant, then the depth to which the weeds grow should also be constant.

- Weed beds do not usually grow in a uniform, straight line Look for pockets, points, and turns, since these will often be the fishing hot spots.

- Weeds that are close to deep water will often produce better fishing than those in shallow water. There are exceptions to this generalization, particularly in fishing for some largemouth bass, but the percentages favor weeds close to deep water.

- Remember that weeds indicate bottom composition. If there is a sudden change from one type of weed to another, it means that the bottom composition has changed, and this means a change in fish habitat.

- Consider the density of weeds. Largemouth bass sometimes move into thick weed beds, but walleyes and northerns avoid them. They are usually found on the edge of a thick weed bed.

- While weeds and a hard rock or gravel bottom don't usually go together, when they do, the combination can result in fantastic fishing. Many older, fertile lakes still have a few small scattered patches of gravel. If you can locate a gravel bar near a thriving weed bed, get ready for some fast fishing.

HOW TO FISH IN WEEDS

There are four basic ways to fish in the weeds: over, under, through and around them.

Al Lindner looks on while Chet Meyers fights a bass that came off the edge of a weedline.

If you are a beginner at fishing the weeds, a good approach is to fish on the edge and around them. Find an area of weeds and then locate the point where the plants stop growing. The outside edge, the edge closest to deep water, is a natural attraction for walleyes and northerns and produces well in the summer. Some weed beds form an inside edge close to shore, and this can be a good fish producer in the early spring.

Position your boat so that you can cast to the outside edge of the weeds and throw your lure or bait as close as possible to the edge. Move your boat slowly down the edge of the weeds, casting just to the edge at all times. Another method is to position your boat right up against the outside edge and cast the length of the weedline.

A variety of lures can be used with either approach, but a jig and minnow combination is hard to beat. The jig and minnow work at all depths and this is important, since the fish locate in different positions according to the weather. On sunny days they may be at the base of the weeds. At other times they may be suspended near the middle, and on rainy, overcast days they may be just below the surface. By staying with the edge of the weeds, you should make some contact with game fish. If you get tired of casting, it is possible to troll the edge of a weedline. Trolling takes patience since weedlines do not run in a straight line, and it usually takes a couple of passes to figure out the points, indentations, and turns.

Fishing over the weeds is an excellent technique, particularly in the spring before weed growth reaches the surface, and in the fall when weeds start to die off. One of our favorite approaches is to locate a fairly dense cabbage bed in the spring of the year that still has two or three feet of open water over the top. Take a lure that dives to the same depth and run it just over the tops of the weeds so that it tickles the topmost leaves. This is a really productive technique for such fish as bass, northerns, and walleyes.

Another technique for fishing over the weeds is to locate a submerged bed of coontail or cabomba. Rig a slip sinker with a floating jig or a crawler that is inflated with air and let out enough line so that the sinker just barely drags over the top of the weeds. Your hook will be floating about a foot above the weeds at just the right level for feeding walleyes and bass.

Fishing under the weeds involves a little more casting skill and finesse than the previous methods. The types of weeds you can usually fish under include a wide variety of lily pads and a few varieties of cabbage that have floating leaves. Here it is crucial to use the appropriate tackle. A weedless hook and fifteen- to twenty-pound test line are almost essential when fishing in the pads. The stems are

This bass came off the edge of a thick cabbage bed and fell to a deep-diving crank bait.

When fishing in thick lily pads, choosing the correct lure is crucial.

tough and the roots deep. Good lures include the Johnson Weedless Spoon and the plastic worm on a weedless hook or one with the hook embedded in the worm. Look for open pockets. Cast into these pockets and, as the lure sinks, begin a slow retrieve. When you hook a fish, don't waste any time getting it out of there. The heavy line will allow you to "horse" it out of the weed jungle into open water.

Another technique for fishing under the weeds is a favorite in the southern states. Locate a thick, floating mat of vegetation over water five to fifteen feet deep. Then poke a hole in the vegetation and, using a jig and eel combination, bounce the lure up and down.

When we fish through the weeds, we are usually fishing through members of the cabbage family. This approach does not work on weeds like cabomba, coontail, and other feathery weeds. Because cabbage is so brittle, however, it is possible to throw a diving plug, complete with treble hooks, into the middle of a seeming "briar patch" and retrieve a lure without bringing in ten pounds of weeds. One technique that is an excellent producer for northerns is to throw a diving plug about ten feet into a cabbage bed and then crank it back to the boat into open water. When the lure hangs up—and you can be sure that it will—give it a hard jerk to free it. Northerns can seldom resist the sight of a struggling lure as it pops off the weeds into open water. Another approach is to cast a jig and minnow into a cabbage bed and work it slowly back through the weeds. Again, if it hangs up, simply tear it free. This means using heavier than normal line, but twelve-pound test is usually sufficient.

GETTING STARTED

Weeds are important habitat for fish for a number of reasons, and since the fish use the weeds regularly, we should learn to do the same. Weed fishing is not as difficult as most people think it is. The biggest problem is overcoming our own hesitancy to fish in the weeds. By learning how to identify some of the basic weed types and by choosing the proper weight line and the best lures for that purpose, you should be able to overcome your natural urge to fish in open water. Since weeds grow to different depths depending on the light penetration and bottom conditions, they should not be associated exclusively with shallow water. Some of the best producers in clear lakes are cabbage beds that grow from twelve to fifteen feet off the bottom.

The weeds will not always hold game fish and, as you learn to fish them, you will soon discover that seasonal patterns and daily weather patterns have an important bearing on their attractions. Still, all in all, they are one of the best places to begin your prospecting. At one time or another, all game fish flee to the weeds for food, cover, or oxygen. Once you discover the pattern for your lake or river, you'll never again curse the lowly water weed.

chapter 4

Weather Watch

How do different weather conditions affect fishing? Are
fish more active when it is sunny or when it is overcast? Is
fishing best when the wind is from the north or from the
south? Do cold fronts really affect fish behavior?

Ask those questions of several anglers, and you will get
quite a few different answers. The only point of agreement
will probably be that weather—any kind of weather—is
sufficient cause for poor fishing. "A cold front hit us, and
we didn't see a fish all day long." "We had to fight a south
wind [or a north, east, or west wind] and got skunked."
While we may not understand very much about the weather, we sure know how to use it to explain our fishing
failures. The problem is that we don't know how and why
fish respond to changes in the weather. They respond all
right, and Chet Meyers has a story about one time they
reacted just like the anglers who were after them.

"It was opening day of largemouth season on Forest
Lake in east central Minnesota. The day was overcast by
the time I got to the lake, and I anticipated a super day of
bass fishing. I rented a boat from the local marina, since
the area I intended to concentrate on was within a few

hundred yards of the marina dock. There were about fifteen boats in the vicinity, but opening-day crowds were to be expected. What was not expected was a sudden southerly wind that came up just as I pushed off from the dock. With the combination of an overcast sky and a gentle wind, my earlier hopes of good fishing soared even higher. I baited up and began fishing the edge of the weedline in about ten feet of water. It wasn't long, however, before my boat had drifted into the thick weeds. I rowed out to the weedline edge and anchored, but now the gentle wind was more like a gale. The waves kept forcing me into shore, and soon many of the other boats began to leave for calmer water. Finally, the last of the other boats left, and I was alone and frustrated. I had rented a boat without a motor, and while others could motor to a protected bay, I had to stick with it or call it a day. After getting soaked by a few whitecaps, I decided that survival was the better part of valor. My only consolation was that I didn't have to row back. I simply lifted my anchor and surfed into the marina channel.

"Thoroughly disgusted with my poor planning and amateur efforts, I rounded the bend into the calm waters of the marina and rowed my boat toward an open slip. As I eased the boat into the dock, I noticed a swirl alongside some cattails on the opposite side of the channel. Intent on not going home skunked, I rowed back out of the slip and tossed a small Rapala close to the cattails. I suspected that there was a school of crappies there, but on the first twitch a three-pound largemouth grabbed my lure and darted under the cattails. I thought the bass I landed was a passing stranger until I saw another swirl. On the next ten casts I landed my limit of largemouth.

"Apparently the fishermen weren't the only ones fighting the wind that day. Largemouth don't like to be rocked around in rough water either, and when the wind got too strong, some of the bass that were in shallow water retreated to the calm water of the marina channel and sought out the cover provided by the floating mat of cattails. They found there not only the protection they sought from the wind, but also an abundant supply of food. The wind had driven schools of shallow bait fish into the same calm water, and those bass weren't about to pass up a free meal."

Every day fish move around in lakes and rivers in response to changes in the weather. The seasonal patterns of location that we discussed in our first chapter help the angler to locate the general vicinity of certain game fish, but once this is determined, it becomes important to understand how fish will respond to daily weather conditions. You may discover, for instance, that a shallow bar with a thick weed bed at its point is a regular gathering place for a school of largemouth bass during the summer, but just where the bass will be on any given day will vary with the weather. On bright, clear days they may be hiding from the sun at the bottom of the weed bed. On overcast days they may move up on the bar and work in toward the shallows. The wind will also affect their location.

Fish behavior is seldom easy to predict. Sometimes it seems that the more we know about fish, the more complex their behavior becomes. While it is dangerous to make generalizations, one rule of thumb seems to have stood the test of time: "The more stable the weather conditions, the more predictable is fish behavior." If you find your school of bass feeding on the west side of that bar in about ten feet of water on a hot, humid evening, chances are that a similar feeding pattern will prevail as long as the weather stays hot and humid. But let a thunderstorm come through, accompanied by a drop in temperature, and those bass will almost certainly move and change their feeding behavior. It is a mistake, however, for an angler to assume that the bass have abandoned the area. The truth of the matter may be that the fish are now feeding in the early morning hours

Two rocky points, one in Canada and one in Illinois. Both may attract fish, but their exact location will be determined by weather conditions.

and that they are on the other side of the shallow bar.

In what follows we are going to look at a few of the more important weather conditions and offer some suggestions for analyzing how weather may affect fish movements on your particular lake or river. We will also look at some angling tactics that will help you cope with adverse weather conditions that usually drive most anglers off the water.

SUN, SUN GO AWAY

Of all the different weather factors that affect fish behavior, the amount of sunlight and depth of light penetration are the most important. While most human beings bask in its warmth, fish view the sun from quite a different perspective. All fish have a strong instinct for survival, and exposure to sunlight means being vulnerable to attack. In a world where one is either eating or being eaten, fish seek out darkness in the form of cover or deep water as a means of escaping other predators.

Several weather conditions control how much sunlight penetrates the water. Cloud cover is one of the more obvious. Usually, the cloudier the day is, the better the angler's chance of locating and catching fish. When skies are overcast, fish move into shallow water to feed, and for most anglers, shallow water fishing is a lot easier than deep water fishing. Not only will fish move to the shallows to feed, they will also remain in the shallows for longer periods of time than when it is sunny. Fish seem to feel safer on overcast days, and divers report that their behavior is not as skittish or cautious. While most people view overcast, drizzly days with dismay, anglers can't wait to get out on the water. They know that their chances of catching fish are much better in a drizzle than when the sun is shining.

Cloud cover, of course, is not the only variable affecting the amount of light penetration. The clarity of the water does much to control the penetration of the sun's rays. With this in mind, it is easy to understand the complaints we often hear from anglers who go north to the lakes of Canada for the trip of a lifetime. "Gee! The weather was just perfect—nice warm sunny days with not too much wind. You couldn't ask for anything better, but the fishing was lousy. Why, we could even see them—big schools of fish—but just couldn't seem to catch any." Every summer the crystal-clear boundary waters of Canada and Minnesota draw thousands of expectant anglers and, sadly, many return home empty-handed. They encounter the worst possible fishing conditions: sunny weather and crystal-clear water. Under these conditions it is difficult for most of us even to raise a fish.

One way the angler can cope with sunny days is to fish early in the morning and towards dusk. An alternative is to avoid sunshine entirely and fish at night. In our travels around the country we are constantly surprised at how few people do any fishing at night. This is unfortunate because almost all species of game fish, except for northern pike, are active and feed at night. Nighttime fishing can be exciting and often yields those lunkers that seldom venture from the depths during the daylight hours.

THE CALM AFTER THE STORM

In recent years the words "cold front" have crept into most anglers' vocabulary, and fishing after the passing of a cold front has become one of the most acceptable excuses for not catching fish. You don't have to be a meteorologist to understand cold fronts—a simple illustration will do.

It is an overcast day, and you have been having pretty good success catching bass off a number of weedy points on your favorite lake. At the end of a fine day of fishing, a cool breeze comes up, and in the distance you see flashes of lightning. That night all hell breaks loose, but by the next morning the storm has passed. The air is cool and dry, and the sun is shining brilliantly. You head out with high hopes and strike out on all your favorite points. You try other approaches. You back troll. You cast. You fish artificials. You use live bait. And at the end of the day, you have a lobster-red face from all the sun and one small bass, which you return so it can grow up. You have just experienced the effects of a cold front.

For years now, anglers have known that the conditions following the passing of a cold front—clear skies and low humidity—mean tough fishing. What they haven't understood is why fishing is so bad and what they can do to adjust to the situation. The reasons behind the "cold front blues" have only recently come to light (no pun intended).

Ron Lindner, Al's brother and executive director of the *In' Fisherman* magazine, has just completed an in-depth study of cold fronts, and his findings should be of interest to anglers everywhere. We have long known that fish associate darkness with safety and for this reason avoid exposure to bright light. But another reason for avoiding light has to do with the effects of ultraviolet rays on a fish's body chemistry. The humidity in the air does much to block out these ultraviolet rays, and it is the combination of intense sun and low humidity that makes a cold front so devastating to fishing. Ron has discovered that fish are not equipped to handle large quantities of ultraviolet exposure. In his own words, "Fish, which have no eyelids, fur, feathers, or clothing, have few options for getting out of the way of these potentially harmful rays. . . . For example, lake trout kept at a proper water temperature but exposed to constant direct sunlight developed cataracts on their eyes in one experiment. In short, fish do not have what it takes biochemically to cope with the effects of ultraviolet rays."

Because their bodies cannot deal with this solar bombardment, fish utilize the only options they have. They move into deeper water or seek cover from the sun. Which option a fish chooses depends on its location as the sky clears and the sun's rays pour into the water. If fish are over a clean bottom with no cover available, they will retreat into deep water. We believe that a good many fish seek out deep water as a primary way of escaping the sun. In areas where cover is available, fish will seek the shade that is provided by vegetation, boat docks, swimming rafts, rocks, and logs. Divers have reported seeing bass actually buried in the weeds with only their tails sticking out.

However well they protect themselves, most fish are adversely affected by the ultraviolet rays that come with clear skies and low humidity. They are in a neutral or negative feeding mood that can be observed in their physical posture. The fish rest very close to the bottom, often with their tails just touching the bottom. Their fins lie back, and it takes a lot of teasing to get them to show any reaction to a bait that they would normally snap up.

Another complication of cold fronts is that fish that have moved to deeper water have thus moved to colder water. The quick temperature change negatively affects the body chemistry of the fish. One final behavior pattern that fish exhibit after a cold front passes through is that they tend to school much more tightly. Loosely scattered schools bunch up like sardines in a can.

With this combination of circumstances, it is no wonder that anglers often fail to catch fish on bright sunny days: the fish are in deep water or under heavy cover, they are concentrated in tight schools, they are not actively feeding, and they are close to the bottom. We know many anglers who even refuse to go out until the third day after a front has passed and things begin to return to normal. Direct observation confirms their caution. Divers report that larger fish are more adversely affected than are smaller fish, and thus they take longer to recover. This is, no doubt, due to the larger body area that is bombarded by ultraviolet

rays. If you happen to be on a weekend fishing trip and a
cold front comes through Saturday morning, however,
there's no reason to turn around and go home. Let's look
at a few ways you can improve your chances.

After the passage of a cold front, walleyes will be hugging the bottom,
and a short snell should be used. When back trolling at moderate
speed, an eighteen- to twenty-four-inch plain snell with leech (1) rides
lowest, about six inches off the bottom. The minnow (2) rides a little
higher, and an inflated nightcrawler (3) rides highest. A six-foot-long
floater rig (4) is much too high at three to six feet off the bottom.

©**In' Fisherman** magazine

- *Change species.* Some game fish are more adversely affected by cold fronts than others. In the northern part of our country, largemouth bass react the most profoundly because of their preference for shallow water. Walleyes are next in line, and northerns seem to be the least affected. If you have your choice of game fish, it makes sense to leave largemouth alone and go after one of the others.

- *Switch to live bait as your primary presentation.* Remember, whatever species you choose, the fish are not likely to be in an active feeding mood. This means that you are going to have to tease them into biting, and live bait will often succeed when artificials fail. We have found that the smaller the bait, the better under these conditions. Small minnows and worms work better than the larger ones we might normally use. One technique that seems to work well on walleyes is to ball a leech up on a hook rather than to let it string out naturally. Rig your live bait as simply as possible. Use light line and a small hook tied directly to the line. Fish close to the bottom, and if you use a slip sinker rig, use a short snell to keep the bait close to the bottom. Since it is crucial to get your bait as close to the fish as possible, a two-foot snell might not work, while a one-foot snell may bring your bait into their range.

- *Use lighter line and smaller hooks than you usually do.* When using live bait for fish that are in a neutral to negative feeding mood, it makes sense to use light line and small hooks. The use of any kind of leader is just about doomed to failure. You may find that you will have to use six-pound test, or even four- or two-pound, before the fish will go for your bait. And a no. 10 hook may look small to you, but many a "cold front" walleye has been caught on one.

- *Try your favorite spots but stay longer and work them over thoroughly.* If you are fairly sure that there are fish in the area and if there is deep water or cover available, stay in one place and work it over carefully. Although we have stressed the importance of moving around, the day after a cold front passes is one time when it pays to sit still. Sometimes still-fishing with live bait is the best approach. While this is not the most exciting form of fishing, it does produce fish under these very tough conditions.

- *Get up close to shallow water stragglers.* While many fish will head for deep water, there will be some shallow water stragglers that will seek the shade of available cover. If you want to try for these fish, getting your bait as close to them as possible is crucial. Here is where pinpoint accuracy in casting can really make a difference. Remember to look for the shady side of structure. In weed beds, expect to find the fish at the bottom of the outside edge in the shade. You may have to make a number of casts to the same spot before a fish will take your bait, so take your time and place your casts carefully. When fishing bass in the shallows, in both the North and the South, we have found that they sometimes move under dense mats of floating vegetation. This can make fishing very difficult, but vertical jigging through this vegetation can sometimes pay off. Again, patience is the key. You may have to jig for three or four minutes in the same place before a bass will strike.

- *If you have a choice, fish the murkier lakes and rivers.* In dark waters, fish are less affected by ultraviolet rays than they are in clear lakes and rivers. The best bet for coping with cold front conditions is to fish a river. For reasons that we don't understand yet, river fish seem to be little affected by cold fronts.

By switching species and adapting your tactics, you can still catch fish like these even after the passage of a cold front.

Although fish are temporarily disoriented by the passage of a cold front, they are usually back in their normal feeding mood within two or three days. The improvement of conditions may not be immediately evident to the angler, but the humidity is increasing and humidity blocks out ultraviolet rays.

If the sun is still shining brightly three days after a cold front has passed, the fish will remain in deeper water. They will be cautious, but they will be feeding, and using normal sunny day tactics should bring results.

FISHING IN THE WIND

Does a wind from the south blow the hook in the mouth? The *Farmer's Almanac* may say so, but for anglers wind is one of the more frustrating forces with which they have to contend. Depending on its intensity, wind can make casting and boat control difficult or can eliminate fishing altogether. At a recent walleye tournament on Lake Mille Lacs in central Minnesota, one of the best walleye and muskie fishermen in the Midwest spent three hours bobbing around in the waves after his boat swamped. The walleyes may have been feeding, but with four-foot waves, not many anglers stayed around to find out.

When a wind comes up, it is important to make quick, sound judgments about the kind of wind and waves your boat can safely tolerate. More than one angler has gone to a watery grave while trying to cross open water in a windstorm. During these times of intense wind, it makes sense to get off the water or seek out those sheltered bays were your safety is not imperiled.

When it is not a hazard to our health, however, wind can improve fishing, both by cutting down on the amount of light penetration and by adding significant amounts of dissolved oxygen to the water. Walleyes, in particular, seem to become very active on windy, choppy days. The added oxygen seems to activate them, and we have had some fantastic walleye fishing when there were whitecaps on the lake. There are other times when wind can frustrate anglers unless they know how to adapt their tactics.

On a recent trip to Ontario, a group of us located a school of walleyes in a narrows at the south end of the lake. It was impossible to discover any feeding patterns because the walleyes hit anything that we threw their way. A few of us even put on some old trout flies with small sinkers and continued to catch fish. That evening a northerly wind came up and blew with a gale force all night long. Towards afternoon on the next day the wind died down, and as soon as it was safe to travel, we headed back to the narrows. After an hour without a fish, it became apparent that something had changed. Luckily, one of our group had a thermometer along and had taken the water temperature the preceding day. When he tested the water again, he discovered that it had plummeted from 64 to 52 degrees Fahrenheit overnight. That twelve-degree drop in temperature had a dramatic effect on fishing. We could only assume that the walleyes had left the narrows or that they were nearby and in a negative feeding mood. Any quick change in temperature upsets the body chemistry of a fish, and it can take a day or two before a regular feeding pattern is reestablished.

It took a while to figure out what had happened, but after we looked at a hydrographic map, it all made sense. The wind that blew the previous night had managed to churn up the lake and bring some of the deeper, colder water to the surface. There was a deep drop-off in front of the narrows, and the wind had blown the warm water out of the narrows and replaced it with colder water. Knowing this and the negative effect it had on the walleyes, we sought out areas of the lake where the water temperature had not been so drastically affected, and we began to catch fish.

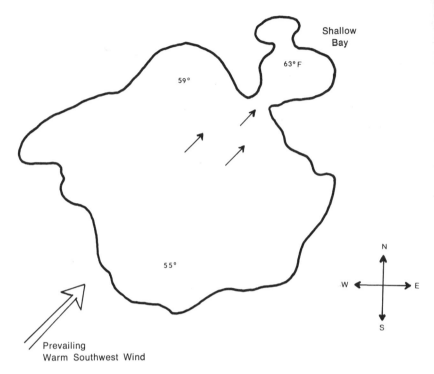

Shallow Bay

63° F

59°

55°

N
W — E
S

Prevailing
Warm Southwest Wind

Warm days in early spring or late fall can move warmer water into a bay like this and increase fish activity.

Sometimes just the opposite effect takes place. In the fall of the year when the lake has cooled off, there will often be a warm sunny day with a slight southerly wind. On these occasions the sun heats the top layer of water, and the wind pushes it into northern bays. The warmth of the water causes the fish to become active and can set off a sudden feeding binge. Reservoir anglers in the South sometimes encounter these warming trends in the middle of the winter, and the smart ones are ready to move to where the warmer water is located.

Wind action can not only bring about sudden changes in water temperature, but it can also affect the movement and distribution of food in a lake. When a lake is under the influence of a wind, there will be a general mixing of the water, but the surface layers are usually those most dramatically affected. Since plankton, small water fleas, and other forms of life at the lower end of the food chain spend most of their time near the surface, it is natural that they are at the mercy of the wind and the currents. As the bait fish follow their food sources in these currents, the game fish follow the bait fish. It may be easier for anglers to fish the leeward side of a lake, but when much of the food is at the windy end, it makes sense to follow the bait fish. While different game fish respond in different ways to these currents, none of them turn down an easy meal if the wind blows it into their mouths.

Roland Martin, one of the best bass fishermen in the country, feels that wind direction and the resulting lake currents are important guides in locating schools of feeding bass. In Roland's experience the bass seem to lie on the edge of a current that is pushing bait fish toward them. Largemouth bass are not adapted to rocking around in waves, but if reasonably calm water is nearby, they will face into the current and feed on available bait fish.

On a recent trip to Table Rock Lake in Missouri with some In' Fishermen staff members, we encountered a perfect example of how wind can affect bass location. Our guide, Dave, was exceptionally good at locating deep water concentrations of largemouth and spotted bass. We had anchored off a likely point in about twenty feet of water and were fishing with night crawlers. We were following a typical summer pattern on Table Rock, but on this particular day the bass just weren't cooperating. There was a slight chop on the water, and Chet noticed the wind breaking around the point with a calm area of water on the opposite side. He suggested moving closer to the point and fishing this current breakline, but Dave insisted that the deep water bass we were after would not be in such shallow water. We fished for another half hour without any luck, and as Dave hauled anchor to move, Chet made his suggestion one more time. Dave shrugged his shoulders and moved the bass boat to within casting distance of the current line. In short order we landed four bass. They were lying right off the point in five feet of water, facing into the current. Dave was a little embarrassed, but he readily admitted that he had not considered the effect of wind on these bass.

While largemouth bass prefer to lie near calm water, walleyes love the rough and tumble action of waves and windblown currents. We have found walleyes feeding in two feet of water with waves crashing around them. On some occasions the wind has been so strong that we have had to beach our boat and cast from the shore into the churning surf. Northerns, on the other hand, prefer calmer waters and avoid wave action. We once found a school of walleyes on the windy side of a point, while fifty feet away on the leeward side we located a school of feeding northerns. When the wind blows, it is important to consider how the fish will respond and be ready to adapt your fishing tactics accordingly. Even a gentle wind creates currents that can cause dramatic changes in water temperature and can move food sources around a lake.

TACKLE TIPS AND BOAT CONTROL IN THE WIND

There are a number of simple tactics that anglers have developed to cope with the frustrations of fishing in a wind. In a strong wind it is important to choose a lure or bait that offers little wind resistance. We suggest using a jig and minnow combination or live bait with a slip sinker. The key to either of these approaches is to use a heavy enough weight so that you can feel some resistance on the end of your line. The biggest problem with fishing in the wind is losing contact with your lure or bait due to slack line. If you can't feel what is going on at the other end of your line, you have lost half the battle. Sometimes this will mean using a one-half ounce or a three-quarter ounce jig or sinker. One-quarter or one-eighth ounce weights are not heavy enough in a brisk wind, and they create so much slack line that you will miss most of the strikes.

Boat control in the wind requires a little versatility. One technique that lets you use the wind to your advantage is called "back trolling." In this approach the motor is put in reverse, and the boat is backed stern first into the wind.

The diagram below shows how the technique works when fishing in a school of walleyes. During the first back-trolling run, contact is made with the fish, and a marker is placed in the water. A run can now be made by back trolling from *B* to *A*, keeping the boat in the fish zone as much as possible. At *A*, the boat is swung around so that the motor points toward deep water. Then the motor is put in neutral, and the anglers move to the other side of the boat. A con-

Back trolling and drifting through a concentration of walleyes, which have just begun to make a feeding movement from deep water.

©**In' Fisherman** magazine

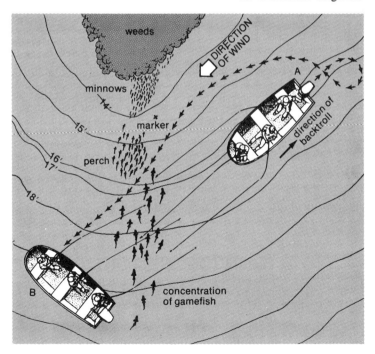

trolled drift is made to *B*. After the boat passes through the fish zone, a straight back troll is made again. Repeat this technique until the fish change position or become spooked.

When back trolling, it is necessary to have some type of splash guards, which are available at most boating stores, to prevent water from washing over the stern. Back trolling is used primarily when fishing live bait and allows for a slow presentation. When back trolling, all of the lines go out the front of the boat, so there is little danger of getting caught up in the motor. Another advantage of back trolling into the wind is that after you have made a pass over a productive area; you can slip your motor into neutral and drift with the wind back over the same spot. This combination of using the motor and the wind to rock back and forth over a school of fish can be a very productive way of catching fish.

There are three basic ways to anchor in a wind. You can anchor from the bow, facing into the wind to prevent waves from slopping into the boat, but the boat is apt to swing from side to side. Although this motion can help you cover a wide area, it can also pull you away from the fish if they are concentrated. Anchoring from the stern reduces swinging, but it is not to be recommended since water is likely to wash into your boat. The best way to stabilize your boat is to use both a bow and a stern anchor. This method has little risk of taking on water and lets you fish downwind over the side of your boat. You might want to experiment with different approaches until you find out which one works best for you. Generally, don't anchor unless you have to. Rather, mark your fish with a marker buoy and then use your motor to keep the boat in position.

FISHING IN THE RAIN

The prospect of fishing in a rainstorm is not very enticing to most anglers. However uncomfortable such an ordeal can be for the angler, most of the time rain does little to disturb the behavior of fish. (In an electrical storm, of course, it is best to get off the water as quickly as possible, since a boat on a lake's surface serves as a natural lightning rod.)

While rain does not always trigger a feeding spree in fish, it happens often enough to risk a few wet clothes. In fact, we have fished in torrential downpours, when it was difficult to see ten feet in front of our faces, and found that northerns and bass almost jumped into the boat.

We don't know why or how the presence of rain affects fish behavior. Some have theorized that during a particularly hard downpour, the beating of the rain on the water's surface helps to oxygenate the water. We do know that rain can wash large quantities of food into a lake or river, and this definitely causes fish to begin feeding. A classic example of this occurrence was reported in a local fishing newspaper a few years ago.

At that time an incredible rain covered much of the middle of the state of Minnesota. The fact that some of the roads were flooded did not stop a local walleye addict from hitching up his boat and heading toward Lake Mille Lacs. This was not the act of a madman but rather, a carefully calculated plan. Many of the sloughs that surround Mille Lacs had filled up, and water started pouring down previously dry stream beds into the lake. With the water from the sloughs came large quantities of leeches, frogs, and worms.

After skirting a police roadblock, our persistent angler (who shall remain nameless) splashed through six inches of water as he followed the road on the west side of the lake to the entrance of one of the larger sloughs. He parked his car and let his boat down right off the edge of the highway. Without moving more than fifty yards from his car, he limited out on walleyes weighing between three and six pounds. He threw back a number of walleyes and northerns and later said that he could see the fish swimming across the highway in order to move farther up the sloughs in pursuit of food.

His extraordinary story points up how runoff from a heavy rain can add new sources of food to a lake's food supply system. Reservoir anglers in the South are well aware of how bass, at the onset of a heavy rain, will move into the coves where small streams enter the lake. Here they not only find a new source of food, but the darker color of the runoff also permits them to move into shallow water without fear of exposure. Trout fishermen and river anglers know that a rising river indicates a rain somewhere upstream and an initial feeding binge by most game fish. Though this increased feeding activity may not last for a long period of time, it can produce incredible fishing while the action lasts.

FISHING BY THE BAROMETER

In doing research for this book we checked our own experience against many books and articles and found little agreement on how barometric pressure affects fishing. Changes in the barometer indicate changes in weather, and for this reason it is important for anglers to watch the barometer. Anglers disagree, though, on how these changes affect fishing. One angler we know of contends that he can predict how and when bass will feed: the lower the barometer falls, the more active the bass. Other knowledgeable anglers hold that just the opposite is true.

We won't side with either of these arguments, but we will make two generalizations that do have solid evidence behind them. First, we have found that fishing can be terrific on a rapidly falling barometer. A drop in atmospheric pressure is often a predictor of violent weather, so if you are fishing during such a time, be on the watch and prepare to get off the water quickly. When the fishing is good, it's all too easy to ignore the weather, as Chet Meyers learned on one of his first fishing trips to the Midwest.

"One afternoon, I was casting for bass in the middle of a small urban lake. Soon the sky took on a strange yellow hue, and a distant siren sounded. Engrossed in my fishing, I didn't notice that all the other boats had left the water and I was alone. I couldn't help but laugh as the fishing got better and better. 'What harm is a little rain going to do?' thought I, and I figured the rest of the anglers were just your average fair-weather fishermen. As a large dark cloud moved overhead, the bass went crazy. I caught and released ten bass on ten casts. Finally the action died altogether, and the sky began to clear. It wasn't until I returned to shore that I discovered I had just witnessed my first tornado warning. I wasn't a smart angler. I was just a dumb Easterner who had never seen tornado skies before."

We are not suggesting such foolhardiness. The only time to fish on a rapidly falling barometer is when there is no danger of tornado, hurricane, or electrical storm. There are times when a falling barometer simply indicates a downpour or the approach of a weather system that will change the present conditions. These can be times of intense feeding, and if it is safe to fish, we would recommend that you give it a try.

The other generalization with regard to barometric pressure comes from research done on largemouth bass by the late Bob Underwood. Using a skin-diving outfit, Bob logged more than 1,700 hours of observations of bass behavior, and during his studies Bob kept careful records of each day's weather and the changes in the barometer. In his book, *Lunker,* he reported that the fish usually paid little attention to his underwater intrusion. In fact, bass and bluegills often swam up to his face mask and gave it a peck. When the barometer began to fall, however, the fish would not let him approach them. Their movements were quick, and their behavior skittish. The fish could still be caught, as Bob's partner on the surface proved, but in order to catch them, he had to make his retrieves with jerky motions that resembled the actions of nervous bait fish.

At first it would seem that these two generalizations are in conflict, but this is not necessarily the case. Since fish are aware of changing barometric pressure and since a falling barometer may indicate the threat of violent weather, it could be that in spite of their anxiety, the fish are eager to feed before bad weather sets in. Small game hunters have noticed similar behavior patterns among rabbits, pheasants, and ducks when the barometer begins to drop. If you decide to fish on a falling barometer, you may find that you will have to vary your retrieve before you hit the right combination. Once you do, get ready for some fast fishing.

THE BEST TIME TO GO FISHING

In the final analysis, most of us go fishing when we have time to fish—we can't wait for the ideal conditions. We can, however, adapt our tactics to the weather, and this is where versatility becomes the key to successful fishing.

In order to fish under different weather conditions, you must know a variety of tactics. A surface lure may work well on a calm surface toward nightfall or in early morning, but it is not productive when whitecaps cover the lake. Casting a jig and minnow is a great technique for walleyes when they are feeding actively, but for "cold front" walleyes, fishing with a light line, a small hook, and live bait is a better bet. By keeping a weather watch and equipping yourself with a variety of tactics, you can find satisfaction in discovering the right combination for even the toughest conditions.

chapter 5

Choosing
a Lake

Every year at fishing clinics we are approached by individuals who pull us aside and open out a hydrographic map of their favorite lake. "Hey! I just happen to have a map here of a lake that I've been fishing for the last ten years. I know there are big walleyes there, but I just can't seem to find them. Would you mind marking a few spots I should check out?" Often, after asking a few questions, it becomes clear that the lake doesn't have a substantial population of big fish. In fact, the lake may not have any big fish in it. When we suggest trying another lake for lunker walleyes, they are disappointed that we can't solve their problems.

Last year Al was in his office when a couple of friends, who are also good anglers, came in to get some information on their particular lake. They had been working this lake for the past four years and had been doing pretty well on walleyes in the one- to three-pound category, but they just couldn't seem to catch any lunkers. They spelled out exactly what they had been doing and then asked Al to suggest some new tactics. Al told them straight out that the problem was not one of proper tactics. This lake just did not produce large walleyes. He went on to say that the lake was one of the best largemouth lakes around, and because most people were busy fishing for walleyes, the bass population was virtually untouched. Our friends weren't using the wrong tactics, they were fishing the wrong species.

Most of us grew up believing that every lake had its monster fish lurking somewhere in its depths. Stories circulated about Old Mossback—the bass that was so old, green moss grew on its back—and Jingle Bells—the giant northern pike that had gotten away so many times that lures dangled from its jaws like tinsel on a Christmas tree. In recent years, we have learned from fish biologists and expert anglers that this just isn't true. Very few lakes produce real lunker fish. Some lakes produce nice eating-size fish, some produce stunted fish, and some lakes don't produce any game fish at all. In most parts of the country we can find examples of

What characteristics will make this a super fishing lake or a complete washout?

each of these types. There are many good fishing lakes, but there are many more that just don't produce large quantities of game fish.

How do you choose a lake that you know will provide good fishing? If you are after really big fish, what type of lake should you be looking for? In what follows we are going to suggest a number of guidelines. Each one tells the angler something about the potential fishing quality of a body of water.

STAYING WITH IT

Before we start making suggestions, however, let's look at the assumption that you should spend your time learning to fish one body of water. Why not skip around and fish a lot of different lakes and rivers? There are a number of reasons to stay with one body of water until you learn it well. We are often tempted to fish a new lake because we hear through a friend that the bass or northerns are hitting like crazy—we can't miss getting our limit. So we pack up our gear and head for that lake, convinced we are going to strike it rich, and we come back skunked.

Did you ever hear the "You-should-have-been-here-last week" stories? Well, many of them are true. As we said in our first chapter, each lake goes through its own seasonal patterns. During each year there will be peak times when the fishing can be excellent on any particular lake. The problem is that by the time word gets around, the fish have usually stopped hitting. Hot streaks on lakes and rivers last a very short time, and trying to catch up with them can be like chasing your own tail. If you should happen to get to one of these lakes during a peak time, you also have to know where to go and what techniques to use. Generally, the only way to profit from this type of fishing is to know someone who fishes the lake regularly and who can not only tell you when to come, but who can also guide you once you get there. This can be a lot of fun, and we have all done it on occasion, but in all honesty what we are doing is fishing on someone else's knowledge.

The real challenge of fishing is learning to locate fish yourself so that you can return the favor and take your friend out on your lake and guarantee good fishing. To do this requires staying with one body of water long enough to learn its different moods and recognize its daily and seasonal patterns.

Recognizing patterns in fishing is the key to success. If you get fish once, you are lucky. If you get them a second time with the same methods, you are on the right track. And if you catch them a third time, you have established a pattern. Where will you most likely find the bass in your lake on a hot, humid afternoon? How deep will you be fishing? Which lures or baits will be the best producers? If you can answer these questions and regularly catch fish, then you know how to identify patterns. If you can't answer these questions, then we would suggest fishing one lake or river until you can. This type of fishing involves a lot of trial and error, but by choosing a good fish-producing lake or river in the first place, you will be able to eliminate a lot of the error and make the trial more fun.

STAYING CLOSE TO HOME

If you are really going to become familiar with fishing patterns in a lake or river, you have to go there often and under a variety of circumstances. That terrific walleye lake in northern Canada that you visit once a year is not a lake you will get to know well. We suggest choosing a lake or river you can reach in less than two hours driving time. It should be close enough so that you can fish it on weekends or even after work. The advantage of such accessibility is that you can watch the weather conditions and plan your angling on the basis of approaching weather.

When choosing a lake, look for one that is close to home. In the early morning anglers are out with the joggers on the shore of Lake of the Isles, within sight of downtown Minneapolis.

Greater Minneapolis
Chamber of Commerce

To get started, pull out a highway map and a compass. Locate your home and draw a circle around it about forty miles in radius. Then locate the area within the circle on county maps that are drawn to smaller scale and look for potential lakes and rivers. Make a list of all the lakes and rivers you want to check out and start exploring.

FISH POPULATIONS

The next consideration in your search for a lake should be to make sure that it has a healthy population of the game fish you want to catch. In most lakes one game fish species is usually dominant. Many northern lakes support a combination of game fish, but even in these lakes one species is dominant. We often refer to such lakes as bass/ northern lakes or walleye/northern lakes with the first species listed as the dominant species. In most southern lakes largemouth bass is the dominant predator, but there are different hierarchies of panfish and bait fish present.

To find out whether or not the species you are after inhabits a given body of water, contact your local department of natural resources. The people there can tell you if the lake has naturally producing fish, or if and when the lake has been stocked. We have a preference for lakes that have a naturally producing population of game fish. Some lakes are both naturally producing and stocked due to heavy fishing pressure. This is good information to know, because a recent study by Ron Lindner has shown that stocked fish often behave differently from those that are naturally produced. In the North, avoid lakes that have a freeze-out every four or five years and that are stocked for interim fishing. The chances of these lakes ever producing big fish is out of the question.

Talk with anglers who regularly fish a lake that interests you. While they may not lead you to their favorite fishing holes, most of them are more than willing to talk about the general quality of the fishing. They might also be able to give you some hints on the seasonal movements on that particular lake.

If it is possible, we would suggest choosing a lake that has two or more species of game fish present. As you fish any lake, you will begin to recognize the conditions that favor one species over another. As we mentioned in the chapter on weather, some species are more dramatically affected by cold fronts than others are. When a cold front comes through and the bass are buried in the weeds, it is comforting to know that there are other fish around, looking for food. Most guides who fish on lakes where a choice is available can tell their clients which fish is going to provide the best action on any given day. We have heard them tell anglers, "Sure I'll take you bass fishing, but we would do much better on walleyes." By choosing a lake with some variety, you will have other options should your favorite game fish be in a negative feeding mood.

LOOKING FOR LUNKERS

Some anglers like to catch a number of eating-size fish, and others are interested only in fishing for lunkers. They would rather catch one 4-pound bass than ten 2-pound bass. They are willing to sacrifice numbers for size. While there is no sure way to guarantee catching lunker fish, you can take a step in that direction by choosing a lake that regularly produces big fish.

In one of the classic studies of growth rates in fish, completed in 1942, Samuel Eddy of the University of Minnesota and Kenneth Carlander of the Minnesota Bureau of Fisheries discovered that growth rates vary greatly from lake to lake. Regional differences, of course, are crucial. A bass in the South grows much faster than a bass in Canada because the growing season is so much longer in warmer climates. By studying fish from lakes in similar

County	Species Studied	Lake Name	Size of Fish	Number of Years for Fish to Obtain this Size
Beltrami	Northern Pike	Big Lake	16 in.	2.8 yr.
		Rabideau Lake	16 in.	3.9 yr.
St. Louis	Walleye	Perch Lake	12 in.	3.3 yr.
		Big Comstock	12 in.	4.7 yr.
St. Louis	Largemouth Bass	Clearwater Lake	9 in.	2.9 yr.
		Fenske Lake	9 in.	5.1 yr.

Comparison of growth rates for the same species in lakes in the same Minnesota county. (Adapted from "Fisheries Research Investigational Report 28," Minnesota Department of Natural Resources.)

counties of Minnesota, the two men eliminated the regional factor and focused on other causes for different growth rates. They discovered that growth also depended on (1) combinations of game fish present competing for food; (2) the overall fertility of the lake and type of prey present; and (3) whether or not the game fish studied were natural to these lakes or stocked. A small part of their study is reproduced above, and indicates clearly that all lakes do not produce big fish.

In fish as in people, growth depends on the number of excess calories consumed, and the number of calories in their diet depends on the type and availability of prey. Some kinds of prey provide more protein and fats than others do.

Species	Age Class Studied	Avg. Length	Smallest	Largest
Largemouth Bass	5 yr. olds	13.03 in.	7.01 in.	20.00 in.
Walleye	5 yr. olds	15.98 in.	12.01 in.	24.02 in.
Northern Pike	5 yr. olds	22.20 in.	15.98 in.	27.01 in.

Comparison of size range from fish of the same age class in various Minnesota lakes. (Adapted from "Fisheries Research Investigational Report 28," Minnesota Department of Natural Resources.)

In many walleye lakes, for instance, perch serve as a primary food source. Walleyes can survive very easily on perch, but they seldom grow as large as ten or fifteen pounds. If, however, walleyes prey on tulibee and cisco, they can become real lunkers. Tulibee and cisco are good sources of protein and fats, while perch have good protein and little fat or oil. So, if you are after big walleyes, it makes sense to choose a lake that also has a tulibee and cisco population. These lakes also produce gigantic northerns. In southern lakes bass grow to the largest size where they have shad as a food source.

Once again, your department of natural resources can tell you what food sources are in a lake. Such agencies do sample nettings of bait fish at regular intervals and are well informed about the food sources that game fish utilize.

Another way to determine if a lake produces big fish is to read the sports page of your local newspaper. Many papers publish a weekly list of large fish and where they were taken. You may find that most of the big fish come out of one or two lakes in your area. And even if you are not after lunker fish, it won't hurt to check with other anglers on the size of fish taken. We know of a lake where we can guarantee you twenty bass on almost any night, and not one of them will be over ten inches long. The fish are stunted because there is just not enough food for them to grow any bigger.

LAKE SIZE AND SHAPE

How large a lake to choose for fishing is, first of all, limited by the type of boat you have. Too many anglers have lost their lives by venturing forth in a boat that is too small for the waves that can come up on big water. Aside from the obvious safety factor, big water can be frustrating to anglers. Big lakes tend to overwhelm us. We don't know where to begin fishing because there is so great an area to fish.

If you do choose a big lake, we would suggest subdividing it into a number of smaller lakes that will be easier to study. By looking at a hydrographic map of a lake and by using natural shoreline boundaries and depth ranges, it is usually possible to break up a large expanse into smaller, manageable areas. Once this is done, stay within the confines of the section you choose and treat it like a separate lake. Be careful, however, of large, shallow bays. Some bays that are gigantic hold fish only during part of the year. To qualify as a "mini-lake," a section of water should have a good depth range and a variety of underwater structure.

Small lakes are usually a lot easier to deal with than

larger lakes. Their seasonal patterns are easy to understand, there is less area to contain fish, and we don't feel over-whelmed by all that water. Small lakes also don't get as nasty in foul weather. There are, however, a few draw-backs. Often, a small lake does not have as large a variety of fish as a large lake. Since it has fewer schools of game fish, it is likely that there won't be continuous feeding. On a really small pond of one or two acres, you may as well pack up and go home when the bass stop feeding. While there is no perfect size, we would recommend choosing a lake that is at least three hundred acres in size. Such a lake is small enough to get to know and yet large enough to pro-vide continuous fishing activity.

One final consideration related to size is the shape of a lake. It makes a big difference if a lake is circular in shape or has an irregular shoreline, especially when a strong wind comes up. We once had three days of fishing completely wiped out because we were on a perfectly round lake when a northwest gale came up. The only place we could fish was near the leeward shore which, in this case, happened to be very shallow with no good holding places for game fish. Whenever we fly into Canada to spend a few days exploring, we look for a lake that has an irregular shoreline featuring extended points and many bays. Then we can find someplace to hold and fish if a wind comes up.

LAKE CONTOURS AND DEPTH

Insofar as possible, narrow down your choice to those lakes that have a variety of structure and good spawning conditions for the species you like to fish. Start your search by obtaining hydrographic maps of the lakes that appear to satisfy your needs regarding location, size, and game fish population. While such maps are somewhat lacking in de-tail, they can give you a fairly accurate picture of a lake's general layout. For most lakes, the maximum depth is

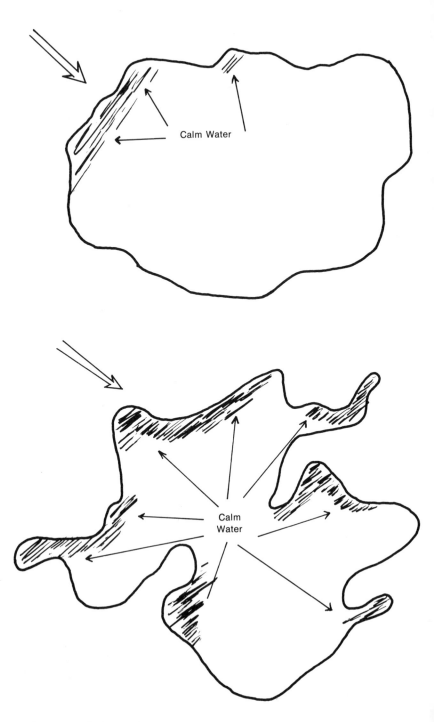

Calm Water

Calm
Water

A strong wind can almost wipe out fishing on one of these lakes,
while the other offers at least a few fishable areas.

marked, and the broad structural contours are outlined.

What should you look for? If your department of natural resources tells you that fish naturally spawn and reproduce in a lake, then check the map for those conditions most likely to foster spawning. For largemouth bass, look for shallow, hard bottom bays that are protected from the wind. If you are after northern pike, then try to locate shallow, weedy sloughs with muck bottoms. Walleyes prefer hard gravel or rubble bottoms with rocks that are fist size or smaller. A few feeder streams attract both walleyes and northerns during the spring spawn. You won't be able to identify spawning grounds until you are actually on the water, but a good map, particularly one that indicates bottom content, can indicate possible locations.

How deep a lake should you choose? If you live in the northern part of the country, we would suggest starting with a lake that has some water in the twenty-five- to thirty-foot range. Initially, it is important to identify underwater drop-offs, points, and sunken islands. Once these are mastered on lakes with a healthy depth range, it becomes easier to recognize the more subtle forms of structure in a shallow body of water. A drop of six to eight feet can be a major fish attractor in a shallow lake, but it takes a keen eye to spot such a break on a depth finder, and few hydrographic maps show them. We feel it is best to start with lakes that have noticeable drop-offs in the five- to ten-foot range and you just won't find these in shallow lakes.

While shallow lakes have their problems, don't give up if they are the only ones available to you. For instance, in the South many natural lakes are very shallow. In these "soup-bowl" lakes, vegetation often becomes the key to locating fish. While visible drop-offs may be rare, a change from one type of weed growth to another constitutes structure and should be checked out. Since most shallow lakes have heavy vegetation growth, you may want to spend some time learning to identify different types of water weeds. Often one type of weed will hold fish, and another will not.

One final consideration is the type of shoreline that prevails on a lake. Where homes or farms border the shore, there is often heavy weed growth due to the use of fertilizers. This weed growth should always be checked out as potential fish-holding structure. Boat docks, swimming beaches, swimming rafts, and rock piles to retard shoreline erosion can all produce fish on occasion. Often, we pass by these obvious hot spots in our search for natural structure.

WATER LEVEL VARIATION AND BEHAVIOR PATTERNS

Most of us don't think of a changing water level as a big influence on fishing, but the level in some lakes changes dramatically, and so does the behavior of the fish that live in them. The key to water level stability in any lake is its water source. The most stable lakes are those that draw their water from the surrounding water table. They are called seepage lakes because the water filters in from the water table, rather than from a river or stream. Seepage lakes seldom have a rapid fluctuation, but a long period of drought or a heavy rain with a lot of runoff can lower or raise the water appreciably. After a two-year drought in parts of Minnesota, many of our lakes were down as much as six feet. During such a drought there is less water and less structure, and the fish tend to concentrate in certain areas. This can make them hard to find but once located, it makes for fantastic fishing. If heavy rain follows a drought and waters rise quickly, the fish will spread out and be difficult to locate until they establish a new pattern.

Lakes that receive their water as part of a river system are called flowage lakes. The water level of these lakes can change quickly. If your lake is a flowage lake, its size may double as a result of a hard rain. The lake assumes the function of a flood plain in a river, and water spreads out everywhere. On the other hand, a drought can reduce a flowage lake to a shallow slough that has little water anywhere but in the main channel. During droughts most fish seek out the channel because it is the deepest water available. They gather in tight schools, and once you locate them, fishing can be excellent. As the waters begin to rise, the fish will once again scatter. When fishing flowage lakes, it is important to learn the patterns that fish exhibit during these fluctuations.

Reservoirs that experience regular drawdowns develop their own fishing patterns. The size of the reservoir can also be important. Sometimes fishing is good during a drawdown, and sometimes it is better when the reservoir is filling up. The only generalization we can make is that the more sudden the change in water level, the more negative the effect on feeding behavior. In large reservoirs drawdowns are sometimes imperceptible and thus have little, if any, influence on fish behavior.

Rivers, naturally, provide the most dramatic examples of water level fluctuation. The extent of flooding in a river depends on the amount of runoff, the number of tributaries, and the age of the river. Young rivers with steep sides and high gradients flood very quickly after a heavy rain. They also return to normal quickly after the rain stops. Fishing is usually good just as these rivers start to rise because a lot of food is being washed into their waters. After an initial feeding binge, the fish become inactive until the river has fallen and is close to normal level. Middle-aged rivers have more tributaries than younger ones and take longer to flood. They also take longer to get back to normal. Again, fishing is usually good as the river begins to rise. Heavy fish feeding continues a little longer than in a young river, and fishing is moderately poor until after the river has begun to fall back to normal. Old rivers vary quite a bit in their patterns. If the river has a good flood plain with lots of standing timber, fishing can be good while the river is rising and even as it reaches its crest. Fish often move into old sloughs and on to the flood plain in search of new food sources.

Each river has a personality of its own, just like lakes, so it is important to learn how your river responds to periods of rain and drought. This takes time, but it is invaluable information. If you fish rivers, you will just have to learn to live with changing water levels. The fish have done it, so can you.

WATER CLARITY

In an age when our national water quality continues to decline, due to industrial and agricultural pollution, most of us tend to associate clean water with clear water. We all dream of those crystal-clear Canadian lakes, where we can dip our hands over the side of the boat and drink the cleanest, best-tasting water in the world. Well, that water may look pretty and may taste good, but it sure is tough to fish. Give most anglers the choice of a crystal-clear lake or a semiclear lake, and they will choose the semiclear lake every time.

Clear water is difficult to fish because of the amount of light penetration. As noted in the chapter on weather, fish generally have an aversion to light. They instinctively associate darkness with safety and avoid exposure to the rays of the sun. Because of these instincts, fish behave differently in clear lakes than they do in semiclear or murky lakes. In clear lakes fish spend most of their time in deep water, venturing into the shallows only when the sun goes down or when the sky is overcast. They may spend most of the day buried in vegetation or in water more than twenty feet deep. If fish are in the weeds, it is necessary to use heavy line. In open water, however, it is important to use line that is light enough so they cannot see it. Light lines and smaller baits seem to produce well in crystal-clear lakes.

In murky lakes fish are not so hesitant about moving into the shallows to feed. Once in the shallows, they spend a much longer time than their kinfolk do in clear lakes. The angler can use heavier tackle, because fish are not as likely to see the presentation.

The weather has a much greater effect on fishing in clear lakes than it does in semiclear or murky lakes. As we mentioned earlier, fish in clear lakes are more adversely affected by cold fronts than fish in semiclear lakes. The best fishing on clear lakes is when the sky is overcast, and there is a good chop on the water. Both of these conditions cut down on the amount of light penetration, making the fish less wary and, therefore, more active.

Water clarity also has an effect on the seasonal patterns of a lake. One of the first In' Fisherman schools was held on Pelican Lake, a crystal-clear lake in central Minnesota. Most of the lakes in this general area were in their summer pattern at the time of the school and were really producing good catches of fish. But in Pelican Lake, fish were scattered all over the place, and it was almost impossible to determine any pattern. The reason was not difficult to figure out once we took its water temperature. Pelican's water was fifty-three degrees Fahrenheit, while most of the other lakes read about sixty-five degrees. The difference was due to water clarity. Clear lakes take a lot longer to warm up than murky lakes do, since they do not absorb as much of the sun's radiant energy. A ten-degree difference in water temperature is enough to put one lake in a peak summer fishing period and another in a tough presummer pattern.

We think it is best to choose a lake with water that is semiclear and has some color. To check the amount of light penetration, lower a reflective white object over the side of the boat on a string. When you can no longer see the object, bring in the string, measure its length, and then double the measurement. (Light must travel down to the object and then return; thus we double the original length.) This will give you the actual depth of light penetration. Another clue to light penetration is the depth to which weeds grow. In some clear lakes, weeds grow to twenty feet before dying out due to lack of light. In murky lakes we have seen weeds stop growing in water over four feet deep.

WATER SKIERS AND ANGLERS

In recent years we have become more and more aware of how intense human activity on a lake or river can cause the fish to alter their normal feeding and activity periods. Many of our best fishing lakes seem to be taken over by water skiers and pleasure boaters. All this water traffic makes fishing difficult and darned unpleasant. Watching a water skier cut off a four-pound bass can drive even a peaceful person to thoughts of murder. With all this competition it is understandable that people aren't catching as many fish as they used to. Soon the fish change their feeding habits, and anglers stop fishing the most populated lakes. In a short time many such lakes get the reputation of being "fished out." More often than not, the fish are there, but they have changed their behavior patterns, as Chet Meyers affirms in this story.

"When I was in college, I worked part-time for the YMCA in a summer day camp for boys. The camp was located on a small lake that supposedly had a good population of largemouth bass in it. On occasion I would sneak away from my duties and try to get in a little fishing, but with the lake crawling with kids—kids swimming, kids turning over boats, kids diving off docks, and kids throwing rocks—I seldom came up with any bass. One day, however, I decided to stay around and get in some evening fishing.

"The scene was quite different. The sun was slowly

It may look busy now, but after the sun goes down, it can be yours alone.

Grand View Lodge, Brainerd, Minnesota

sinking, and there wasn't a sound in the air, except for a bullfrog who was just a little ahead of schedule. After the noise and bustle of the day, the lake lay calm, seemingly glad for the tranquil night that lay ahead. I tied on a Jitterbug and threw it out alongside the swimming dock. On the second twitch I was fast on to my first bass of the evening. About ten minutes later another bass inhaled my lure and still has it, for all I know. I finished the evening with six bass weighing between one and three pounds, and I was both delighted and surprised by my catch. It seemed that because of the small size of the lake and the intense activity during the daylight hours, the bass had adapted their habits to those of the campers. When the kids hit the lake in the morning, the bass dropped off into the deep water in the middle of the lake. And when the kids went home, the bass came out to play."

The shallower the lake and the more intense the human traffic, the more radically the fish will alter their habits. The only way to catch fish on these lakes is to adapt your fishing tactics by fishing early in the morning and late at night. Fishing may also be productive in the spring and fall when boaters and skiers are not on the water.

Many anglers give up on urban and resort lakes and push farther on into the wilds. It's too bad, because many of these lakes still provide excellent fishing. Some of the best bass lakes in Minnesota are within the city limits of Minneapolis and Saint Paul. Similarly, some of our heaviest-used vacation lakes still have huge populations of walleyes and northerns. One of the best walleye lakes in the state is considered "The" vacation lake for boaters, skiers, and drinkers. The lake suffers little if any serious fishing pressure, and yet it harbors one of the best populations of lunker walleyes in the state. Only a few anglers fish this lake, and they aren't saying much—they have it all to themselves when the sun goes down.

chapter 6

Fishing
a New Lake

It was one of the first warm evenings of a long-awaited spring. The sun was sinking slowly, and a fine layer of clouds near the horizon helped turn the sky into brilliant shades of red and orange. Chet Meyers and his father were fishing a small lake less than a mile from the heart of downtown Minneapolis.

"Suddenly, the calm of the lake was shattered as a northern pike exploded under Dad's jointed minnow lure. The strike blasted a hole in the surface of the water as if a small underwater mine had just gone off. Dad led the fish by the boat, and I scooped up a healthy five-pound northern. As I was busy putting the fish on the stringer, Dad let out a whoop, and the bend in his rod indicated another nice fish. A few minutes later a seven-pound northern joined the first on our stringer. Then, as quickly as it had started, the action ceased.

"We tried to relocate the school, but they had probably been disturbed by the action of landing the two previous fish and were no longer feeding. Most of our fish go back into the lake, but since we had promised some friends a dinner of northern, deep-fried in beer batter, these two fish would fill the bill. As we pulled into the dock, an angler who was casting from shore stopped by to chat. 'Nice fish you got there,' he said. 'You guys must know this lake pretty well. Don't often see fish that size come out of here.' We talked awhile, explained where we had caught the fish, and then added that this was our first time out on the lake. 'Boy! That's what I call luck,' the man muttered as he moved down the shore to resume his casting."

There are few thrills that compare with going out on a new body of water for the first time and discovering its patterns—not just catching some fish, but learning the pulse of that lake and understanding why you caught those fish. Anyone can "luck into" some fish, but the skilled angler relies on well-planned tactics to fish a new lake.

During the fishing schools that the In' Fisherman runs each summer, we have all our participants complete an exercise called "psyching out a new lake." The exercise involves collecting information on a lake or river similar to the information outlined in the last chapter. The anglers use a chart like the one on page 95 to organize the data, which they keep in their tackle box. Most of this information can be gathered before you ever set eyes on that new lake you want to fish. And, when you put this information together with a systematic set of tactics, you can almost be guaranteed a better-than-even chance of landing some nice fish in a very short period of time.

THE SURVEY

The biggest mistake that most anglers make when fishing a lake is that they start fishing immediately. That may sound like a crazy statement, but it's true. By spending some time surveying the lake so that you can use a methodical approach to fishing it, you can save countless hours of frustration. The survey comes first. There will be plenty of time for fishing later.

Lake or River Name __Bass Lake__ No. of Acres __323__

Location __East Central Wisconsin__

General Depth Range/Structure __Fairly Shallow, 34' Max. Depth, not much structure__

General Physical Shape __Irregular, 3 small bays, North/South Axis__

Type of Shoreline __Combination Marsh & Woodland - small public swimming area.__

Predominant Bottom Composition __Sand, hard mud, and muck__

Water Level Fluctuation __Stable seepage lake, no permanent inlets/outlets__

Normal Water Clarity __About 12 feet__

Vegetation Present & Normal Summer Weedline Depth __Coontail, Cabbage, Lilypads__

Gamefish Present __Bass dominant species (naturally producing), some pike stocked__

Forage Present __Crappies, bluegills, bullheads, some carp (test netting - Aug. 1975)__

Fisheries Management __Northerns stocked 1975 - 2000, 1971 - 3500__

Human Usage __Swimming beach, N.E. End__

Other Observations __Most of east shore wooded except for a few homes,__
__Large bar & one sunken island not indicated on map__

Information chart.

©**In' Fisherman** magazine

Let's assume that you have collected all the information about a new lake that you can before visiting it. Arm yourself with extra copies of your hydrographic map and a depth finder. A good depth finder not only indicates exact depths so that you can discover bottom contours, it also picks up vegetation and helps you determine the composition of the bottom. With a little practice, the depth finder will become a set of underwater eyes that you can rely upon. One final tip—a pair of Polaroid sunglasses allows you to see beneath the surface of the water so that you can spot shallow underwater structure and vegetation that grows to within a few inches of the surface.

The steps of the survey itself are as follows:

- *Check the clarity of the water.* Estimating the amount of light penetration gives you a key to the depth of the weedline on the lake. The clearer the water, the deeper the weeds will grow.

- *Run the entire shoreline of the lake.* Use the depth finder to check the accuracy of your hydrographic map and look for structure that is not indicated on the map. Start your survey at the first major drop-off. If the lake is fairly shallow, then locate the outside edge of the weedline and use this as your guide. Look for boat docks and other man-made structure, visible weed beds, and other clues along the shoreline. A steep shoreline usually means deep water close to shore. Points often extend out into the lake as bars. Cattails on a shore usually mean a muck bottom. Mark all such points of interest on your map. During the survey the boat can be run fairly fast. If possible, do the survey with a friend so that one of you can operate the motor and the other is free to observe the shoreline and mark the map.

- *Run a crisscross or checkerboard pattern across the middle of the lake.* Your purpose here is to locate bars or sunken islands that the original mappers missed. On a narrow lake zigzag back and forth down its length, and on a circular lake run a checkerboard pattern. Check the contours given on the map against the readings of the depth finder.

- *Estimate the seasonal pattern of the species you are seeking.* Take the water temperature and apply what you have learned about fish behavior on lakes similar to this one in terms of seasonal patterns. Only time on the water and a log of your trips will enable you to pinpoint patterns on a particular lake, but some generalized knowledge will help you pick a likely spot to begin fishing.

The survey we have described usually takes less than an hour. Generally, lakes that are five hundred acres and smaller can be "psyched-out" in one trip. If your lake is bigger than this, do as we suggested earlier. Break it down into manageable sections and learn one section first.

To illustrate the process of learning a new lake, let's survey a small bass/northern lake. The lake is actually a composite of several new lakes that we have surveyed over the years. The lake—we will call it Bass Lake—is just a little over three hundred acres. Map 1 on page 98 shows its depth range as plotted by the surveyors. Our first trip around the perimeter of the lake might reveal the following points of interest, as shown in map 2, page 99.

- *Point A:* a shallow bay that we mark down since it looks like a potential spawning bay for largemouth bass.

- *Point B:* a departure from the hydrographic map. It is a small, weedy point that could hold bass or northerns.

- *Point C:* the western shore of a large bay that forms a flat, hard-bottomed shelf, which is perfect for bass spawning. As we motor by, we can even see the saucerlike depressions where bass spawned a few weeks earlier.

- *Point D:* a weed bed composed of broadleaf cabbage.

- *Point E:* a clean gravel bar, not far from the weed bed at point D. This combination of gravel and weeds is often a super fish producer.

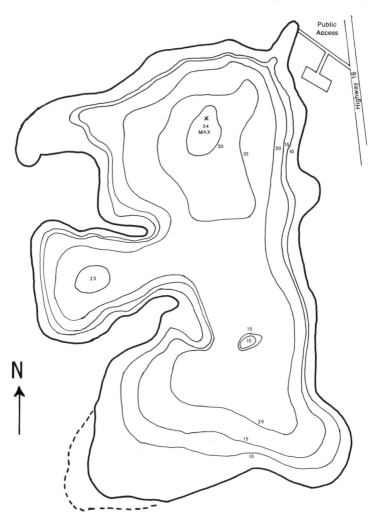

Bass Lake, map 1.

- *Point F:* a muck bottom that is only five feet deep. According to the map we should be in twenty feet of water, while this whole end of the lake is actually very shallow.

- *Point G:* some lily pads that look as if they may hold bass.

- *Point H:* another departure from the map. Our boat is in three feet of water instead of the fifteen marked on the map. We suspect that there is a large bar here.

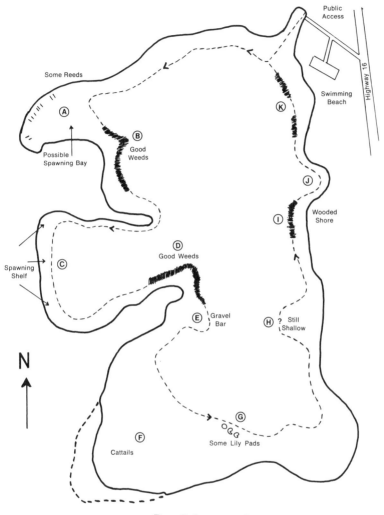

Bass Lake, map 2.

- *Point I:* a very thick bed of coontail mixed with cabbage.

- *Point J:* an area almost fifteen feet deep that is shown on the map as a shallow bay.

- *Point K:* a place near the swimming beach where some-one has raked the bottom clean of weeds. While this is poor ecology, it does produce a break between weeds and hard bottom and often attracts fish.

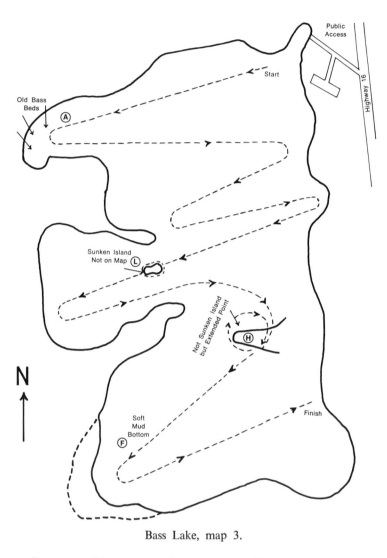

Bass Lake, map 3.

Because of its narrow shape, we would run a zigzag pattern across Bass Lake to discover what is in the middle of it. Map 3, above, indicates some things that few people would discover unless they took a survey such as ours:

- *Point A:* Just to check on our earlier hunch, we motor into this bay and learn that the bay is peppered with bass and bluegill spawning beds.

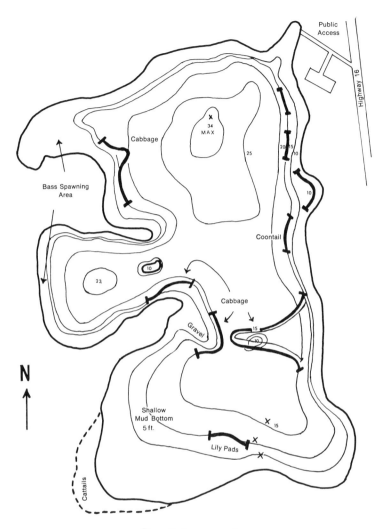

Bass Lake, map 4.

- *Point L:* Here we discover a small sunken island that comes to within ten feet of the surface. Since it is covered with coontail and cabbage, it looks like a dynamite place for both bass and northerns.

- *Point H:* As we had suspected, this is a gigantic bar that almost cuts the lake in half. Its presence explains the sunken island indicated on the orignal map. Apparently the original surveyors did not do a thorough job of mapping depths at this end of the lake. They must have assumed that shallow water this far from shore would be a sunken island.

- *Point F:* To check out our earlier observation, we run as close to shore as we can. The entire area is shallow and mucky with little, if any, good weed beds. As a result, we can write off one huge section of the lake.

After completing the survey, we would make our final corrections on one map, map 4, page 101. One look at the map shows us that we have probably eliminated 75 percent of the lake as fishless water. Thus we can concentrate all our time and effort on the remainder, and in so doing we will be fishing close to 80 percent of the fish. Playing the percentages in this way just has to improve fishing success.

Now, before actually rigging up, all we need to consider is the seasonal pattern of the game fish we are after. Let's stay with Bass Lake as an example and assume that we are going to concentrate on fishing for largemouth.

In southern Minnesota, largemouth move into their spawning areas when the water temperature gets into the high fifties. They spawn at about sixty-two degrees Fahrenheit. If the water temperature in Bass Lake is still in the low sixties when the bass season opens, we should look for bass near points A and C, since we know from our survey that these two places hold bass during spawning. Spawning areas for bass change little from year to year unless the water level drops or rises significantly. If the water temperature is close to seventy degrees, then we may assume that the bass have abandoned their spawning areas. After the spawning season, weedy points such as B and D might be good spots to start fishing. Sunken islands, such as L, are almost always good summertime producers. If we are fishing in the fall, when the water temperature has dropped back

down into the fifties, the bass will be less active. We would
expect to find them near the deeper water, such as the slot
between points H and E, and we would also look for them
near point K. Steep drop-offs are usually good producers
in the fall of the year.

NOW IT'S TIME TO START FISHING

If you are like most of us, by the time you have completed
the surveys and picked out potential fishing spots, your
adrenaline is pumping like crazy. For actual fishing tactics,
choose methods in which you have confidence and which
are appropriate for the fish you are after. Here is where
fishing with a friend is really helpful. You can increase
your odds of success if each of you chooses a different bait
or lure. By offering the fish a choice between a crank bait
and a plastic worm and by changing lures when your first
choice fails, you will have twice as many chances to discover
what the fish are after on any given day. If one of you
starts catching fish regularly, then it's time for the other to
switch to the lure or bait that is producing.

Begin your fishing by choosing the spot that looks the
most productive. You should have at least a dozen spots
marked as a result of your survey, so if one doesn't produce,
you know where to go next. The time you spent doing the
survey can actually save you hours of motoring aimlessly
around a lake. Work a spot thoroughly with different lures
and tactics, but if you strike out, move on to the next. Fifteen minutes is usually plenty of time to see if any fish
can be triggered into striking.

Keep moving and looking for a pattern. If you catch
fish near a thick cabbage bed, locate other such weed beds
on your map and fish them. Consider the position of the
sun and the shadows it casts on the water and pay attention
to wind direction. If a likely spot doesn't produce, come
back to it later. The fish may be moving around and stop-

Al Lindner works a largemouth bass out of heavy timber while fishing a strip mining pit near Brainerd, Minnesota.

ping temporarily to feed elsewhere. Be sure to mark down on your map the areas where you caught fish. Indicate in your log what lure or bait you were using and the depth at which you caught the fish.

If your first trip is not a big success, don't despair. Every lake has its on-and-off days. For some, the time of day is important. If you fished from sunup until noon and got skunked, plan to fish from noon until sundown the next time. Once you have identified those locations that produce fish, keep coming back to those spots, but don't fish them exclusively. Check out the depths every time you are on the lake. If you discovered one sunken island on your first survey, there are probably other smaller ones that are waiting to be fished. Change your location, change your tactics, and relocate the fish. Keep at it. Fishing in a logical, systematic manner is bound to pay off, and when it does, you'll never feel lost on an unfamiliar lake again.

chapter 7

Tools
of the Trade

"When I was a child," Al Lindner remembers, "I spent
hours looking at the strange and wonderful lures in my
father's tackle box. Their shapes and colors intrigued me,
and the teeth marks that they bore started my imagination
running wild. Some seemed so large that I had difficulty
imagining any fish swallowing them. There were many
lures in that old rusty box, and a few of them were treated
with special reverence by my father. Their painted wooden
bodies were chipped and well scarred, but to Dad they
seemed to possess a magical quality. I became even more
aware of how special these lures were when I began joining
my father and his friends on their fishing trips. More than
once I dove into cold water or climbed a pine tree to retrieve a lure that most anglers would have written off as
lost."

Many of us never lose that childlike fascination for pretty
colors and strange shapes, for each spring we migrate to
the local tackle stores to see what new lures are on the
market. It seems that in the past few years there has been
an explosion in the tackle industry. During a recent trip
to a nearby store we counted more than one hundred and

fifty different styles and sizes of lures. It is no wonder that many anglers are confused about which lures will best serve their purpose. And, to add to the confusion, each year sees the arrival of a new lure that promises to solve all our fishing worries. We have all probably been conned by the "magic lure" gimmick, but sooner or later, we come to realize that the only thing those lures consistently catch are anglers looking for easy answers. There simply isn't now—nor will there ever be—one lure that always puts fish on the stringer.

While there may not be any one magic lure, there certainly are types of lures that produce better than others under a given set of circumstances. In this chapter we'll be making suggestions about the types of artificial lures that every angler should know how to use. We do not believe that it is necessary to have a tackle box the size of a footlocker in order to accommodate such a selection. What is crucial is not how many lures you own, but how versatile your selection is. The contents of your tackle box should enable you to deal with almost any fishing condition.

CHOOSING LURES THAT RUN AT THE PROPER DEPTH

Many of us have wished that we could slip over the side of the boat, put on a diving mask, and check out the area we are going to fish. According to Jeff Zernov, a fisherman who also does a lot of diving and underwater photography, if we could see all the fish that are under and around our boat, it would probably put an end to our fishing for the day because of sheer frustration. Often, he has seen lures only two or three feet above or below schools of game fish that will not move to attack it. The angler was fishing at the wrong depth.

One thing we have learned in recent years is that game fish do not like to expend a lot of energy to chase down a meal. Although a northern pike will sometimes follow a lure for ten or twenty yards before striking, most of the time fish are hesitant to move even a few feet to take a lure or bait. Another thing we have learned from fish biologists is that fish spend most of their time in an inactive state. We estimate that they are feeding actively only 5 to 10 percent of the time. The rest of the time they are either in a neutral feeding mood (80 percent) or a negative one (10 percent). The closer you put your lure to the fish, the better your chance of filling out your stringer. The first thing to do is to fish at the correct depth. A painful illustration from a fishing trip Chet Meyers took recently should help make the point.

"Last year a friend and I were fishing a bass lake close to my home. We had gone out after dinner, and since we only planned to fish for two hours, we grabbed a few lures and left our tackle boxes at home. I started out using a shallow diver that went to about three feet. Ron was using a spinner bait and working it just off the bottom. We fished around the weeds, and before the sun went down, I had four bass while Ron had managed to land only one. We decided to head in since the mosquitoes were nagging us and it was getting dark. As we moved toward the dock, Ron suggested making a few casts around a weedy point that was in about six feet of water. On his first cast he connected with a small bass. It was not until Ron had landed three bass in quick succession that I realized he was picking them up right off the bottom. My lure was running only three feet deep— and three feet over the top of those bass. Being a gentleman, Ron tossed me an extra spinner bait, and I caught a bass on my first cast. Before sunset, my shallow diver had been doing pretty well because the bass were at the three-foot level. When the sun dipped under the horizon, the bass dropped down deeper, and my lure was ineffective. Three feet made all the difference in the world."

When most of us check out a particular area for fish, we tie on our favorite lure and make about fifteen casts. If we don't catch anything, we conclude that either the fish aren't biting or that they have gone elsewhere. Now either of these alternatives may be true, but it is also possible that the lure or bait was not within the proper range of the fish. We suggest that you always try to work an area at two or three different depths before moving on. To do this, you will need an assortment of lures that can be worked at different depths, and you will have to know how to use them. Often, an adjustment of two or three feet can spell success instead of failure.

Most of us were brought up to think that the really good anglers were the ones who could cast a lure a hundred yards and land it on a dime. We thought that casting accuracy was the key to success. Casting accuracy is still important, especially when you are fishing surface lures and need to lay a cast close to a stump or under an overhanging tree, but as we suggested in chapter 2, throwing surface plugs at shoreline structure is spending a lot of time on very few fish. Generalizations are always dangerous to make, particularly about a sport like fishing, but we will venture one that has a lot of truth behind it: Most of the time, in most lakes, most game fish will be in water deeper than five feet.

Now ask yourself this question and answer honestly. How much time do you spend fishing in water more than five feet deep? If you are like most anglers, the answer is, "very little." The boat may be in deep water, but seldom do our lures work below the five-foot level. In what follows we are going to make some suggestions about the types of lures that you should know how to use. Our assumption is that the versatile angler knows how to work from the surface all the way down to the bottom. While there may be hundreds of lures to choose from, all you really need are a few lures in each of the following categories. We will start at the surface and work our way down.

SURFACE LURES

Fishing surface lures is one of the great joys of angling. There is no greater thrill than when the soft gurgle of a surface plug being drawn over the placid water of a lake is interrupted by a bass launching its attack. No matter how many years of experience we have had, the suddenness and the fury of such an attack still leaves most of us with shaking knees.

Every angler should know how to fish at least one of the many effective surface lures that are on the market. These lures are designed to float while at rest and to create some disturbance when they are retrieved. Some gurgle, some sputter, and some make popping noises, but all are designed

Surface lures (top to bottom, left to right): Hula Popper, Super Frog, Crippled Minnow, Jitterbug, Crippled Minnow.

to get the fish's attention. They are primarily designed for fish that at times feed on the surface. Largemouth and smallmouth bass, northern pike, muskie, and chain pickerel are their most common target, though we once heard of a deranged walleye that succumbed to a Jitterbug. The key to fishing these lures is in the retrieve. Most anglers swear by a stop-and-go method in which the lure is alternately retrieved and rested. These lures are best fished over heavy cover such as the tops of weed beds or near the tops of sunken bushes and trees. They operate best when the water is a flat calm.

Three of the more popular models include the Jitterbug, the Hula Popper, and the Crippled Minnow. With the use of a fly rod there are innumerable flies and popping bugs that work well on both bass and members of the pike family. We would suggest trying out a few models and then choosing the type you have confidence in. Buy a few different sizes and colors, but stay with one model until you really learn how to fish it.

One major problem with surface lures is that they are too much fun to fish. Sometimes this really limits an angler's versatility. We know some who say they would rather catch one bass on a surface plug than ten on an underwater lure. At this point they aren't contesting a lure's effectiveness; they are simply stating an esthetic preference. We agree that for lasting memories, nothing can touch surface fishing, but for all-around effectiveness, it is a limited approach.

SHALLOW DIVERS

Shallow divers run anywhere from one to seven feet in depth. They float at rest and usually work with a side-to-side wobbling motion when retrieved. Some shallow divers run only at a given depth no matter how fast they are reeled in. Others work deeper if they are retrieved quickly.

There are two basic types of shallow divers. The first

Shallow divers (top to bottom, left to right): Floating Rapala, Big O, Bass-O-Reno, Pikie Minnow, River Runt, Swimming Mouse.

runs very shallow, reaching a maximum depth of three feet. These lures are great for fishing over the tops of weed beds in the early spring, before they are fully grown, and in the fall, after the weeds have begun to die off. Since most fish at some time seek out the weeds for food or cover, a lure of this type is an important one to have in your tackle box, These lures are also useful for checking out shallow water in the early morning or in the evening. Examples in this category include the Floating Rapala, the Swimming Mouse, and the Bass-O-Reno.

The second type of shallow diver is a lure that runs from three to seven feet in depth. Many lures fall into this category, but in recent years a series referred to as crank baits or alphabet plugs seem to be fairly successful. They were originally developed in the South and are excellent for use on largemouth and smallmouth bass. The Big O, Big N, Bagley B, and other fat, tight-wobbling lures are examples in this series. Since their introduction in the South, many anglers in Canada and the northern United States have found that they work well on northern pike and occasionally on walleyes. Crank baits work well on gradual drop-offs and the edges of shallow weedlines. One method is to cast the lure a few feet behind the outside edge of the weeds and then to "rip" the lure through the remaining weeds into open water. A fish will often hit the lure just as it tears loose from the weeds. Crank baits usually work best when retrieved as fast as possible. Don't worry about the fish not being able to catch it. When a fish decides to attack, no lure is going to escape.

In addition to these newer models, there are the old standbys that have been around for decades. The River Runt and Pikie Minnow are only two of the many divers that will reach the three- to seven-foot level. These lures can be both cast and trolled. Again, we would suggest that you choose one or two models and then get that particular model in a few different sizes and colors. Some days green will work best, and other days the fish won't hit anything but fluorescent orange.

MID-TO-DEEP DIVERS

This is a kind of catch-all category, in which we have included any plug that can normally be fished in water deeper than seven or eight feet. If you are casting these lures, you probably won't reach much deeper than fifteen feet. If you troll them, they will run somewhat deeper. The deep divers are designed to scrape along the bottom or work down the sides of steep embankments. They are great for fishing around rock piles since their big lip prevents them from hanging up. Some crank baits, such as the Deep O and Deep N, come in deep-diving models, which have a

Deep divers (top to bottom, left to right): Hellbender, Bomber, Deep O, Spoonplug.

larger diving lip. Generally, the instructions will tell you how deep the lure is designed to run.

Within this category we also find a series of lures that have been designed primarily for deep water trolling. Three of the better-known lures in this series include the Bomber, the Hellbender, and the Spoonplug. You can purchase them in sets of five or six. The smaller sizes run shallower than the large size. Fishing these lures properly is an art form all its own called speed trolling. The lures are designed to be trolled very fast, twice as fast as you would normally troll a lure. You need a very stiff rod and a large capacity bait-casting reel with twenty- to thirty-pound test nonflexible line. The novice angler seldom speed trolls, but the lures can also be cast and work very well in fishing steep drop-offs. If you are trying speed trolling for the first time, talk with someone who has done it before and get ready for a challenge. Sometimes just holding the rod with the lure on it becomes a battle in itself.

JIGS

The lowly jig is probably the most underrated lure in our tackle boxes, and yet it is one of the most versatile. The powers-that-be in the U.S. Navy must think so, because a jig is included in all of its basic survival kits. Entire books have been written about jig fishing, and we aren't about to duplicate all of that material. The important thing for most anglers to realize is that each type of jig has a slightly different function and that the shape of the jig determines that function. Round-headed jigs are designed for fishing over

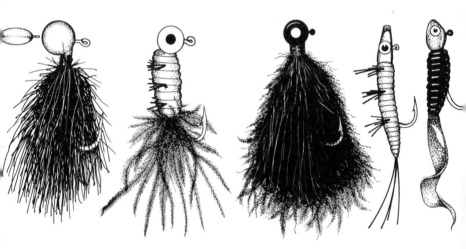

Jigs (left to right): narrow head with bucktail, rubber grub body with marabou feathers, ball-type body with marabou feathers, Gapen's Ugly Bug, and jig with plastic twister tail.

©**In' Fisherman** magazine

clean bottoms. Jigs with offset eyelets work well on rocky bottoms, particularly rivers, where the offset creates a level effect so that the lure can be tipped over rocks without hanging up. Thin-shaped jig heads are designed for fishing in the weeds. The thin shape helps the jig slide down between the weeds with a minimum of disturbance.

No matter what its function is, the purpose of a jig is to get to the bottom quickly, and often that's where the fish are. An additional benefit is that jigs can be fished in combination with live bait without destroying their action. Often, a jig that is tipped with a minnow or a piece of nightcrawler really turns the fish on.

The action of a jig is totally dependent on the angler. It can be reeled in with a skipping motion, thus imitating a crayfish on the bottom. It can be worked from side to side in a swimming motion. Or it can be retrieved without any movement at all. Many different types of motion can be imparted to jigs. Another nice thing about jigs is that they are relatively inexpensive, and you can save even more money by making your own. If you are unfamiliar with the different types of jigs and their functions, your sporting goods dealer can usually help out. We suggest that you get an assortment of weights and colors. Weights can be particularly important when fishing different depths or when river fishing.

SPOONS AND SPINNERS

The spoon is probably the oldest fishing lure known to man and has been found in some of the oldest prehistoric ruins. Spoons can be fished at any depth, depending on the speed of the retrieve. Many anglers, however, never work a spoon more than a few feet under the surface because they begin to reel it in immediately after the cast. An angler who is fishing in twenty feet of water may think that the spoon is down deep, but due to their construction, spoons ride up very quickly. Just as in fishing any other lure, it takes a little practice to learn how to use a spoon properly and to fish it at various depths. Spoons can be bounced off the bottom like a jig, retrieved through the mid-depths, or even skimmed over the surface.

On a recent trip to Canada, a group of us flew into a remote lake known for its walleyes and northern pike. We stayed a week and caught a lot of nice walleyes but couldn't locate any northerns bigger than five pounds. On the flight out, we asked the pilot if he knew of anyone who had ever done well on big northerns in that lake. He told us he did, but said that we wouldn't believe him because the man's technique was so strange. He consistently went home with his limit of fifteen- to twenty-pound northerns and threw a lot more back. He owed his success to trolling a very large

Spoons and spinners (top to bottom, left to right): Daredevle, Red Eyed Wiggler, Johnson Weedless, Mepps Spinner, Shyster, Panther Martin.

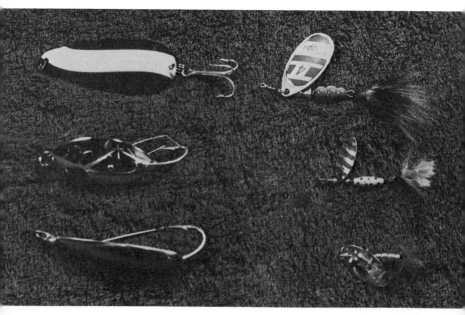

Daredevle behind his boat so fast that the lure just skipped over the surface. He used a fifteen-foot sturdy cane pole and about thirty feet of thirty-pound test line. The boat was run close to shore with the pole fully extended towards the reed beds. When a northern struck, he would set the hook and then throw the cane pole overboard. Then he would circle back and follow the pole around until the fish tired itself out.

Our pilot was right. We didn't believe him until we checked the story out with some other anglers who knew of this technique and swore by it. We seldom think of fishing spoons on the surface, but it does produce. By beginning your retrieve before the spoon hits the water, you can keep it skimming over the top of the water. This is usually a northern pike technique, so be prepared for a big strike. It can almost tear the rod out of your hands.

A number of the more popular spoons include the Daredevle, the Red Eyed Wiggler and the Johnson Weedless Spoon. The Johnson Weedless should be in everyone's tackle box because it can be worked in the thickest weeds imaginable, and does it catch fish!

Along with a wide variety of wobbling spoons, there are a large number of spinner spoons available. The spinner has a rotating blade and a weighted body and works for just about any game fish species. The biggest problem with spinners is that they are apt to twist one's line. Though we most often suggest tying your lure directly to your line, it is wise to add a small ball bearing swivel when fishing a spinner. A few spinners that have an offset eyelet can be tied on directly. As with the wobbling spoons, spinners can be fished at any depth. They work as well in clear water where their flashing motion is a fish attractor as in murky water where the whirring sound attracts a fish's attention. A few popular spinners include the Abu Reflex, the Mepps, the Panther Martin, and the Gladding Shyster.

SPINNER BAITS

The spinner bait became popular about ten years ago, and when it first hit the market, it caused quite a stir. By now it is found in almost every tackle box. Some people refer to the spinner bait as a safety pin lure because its shape resembles an open safety pin. It is probably the most versatile lure in existence since it combines the best features of a jig, a spoon, and a spinner, and in addition it can be used with live bait. It usually has a large single hook that rides in an upright position. This adds to the lure's versatility by making it almost weedless and snagproof.

Spinner baits usually come with a rubber skirt, a bucktail, or some other artificial dressing over the hook. Live bait can be added to the hook without disturbing the

Spinner baits (left to right): single spin with rubber skirt, tandem spin, single spin with bucktail skirt.

balance or action of the lure. Some anglers tie on an additional hook to the main hook to catch fish that are striking short. Spinner baits with one blade or two tandem blades are available. The tandem spins have a tendency to ride to the surface quickly, but they are a most successful shallow water lure for muskies and big northerns.

As with many other lures, the action of a spinner bait is pretty much determined by the angler. It can be skipped across the bottom like a jig, fluttered through the mid-depths, or buzzed over the surface. The most common mistake that anglers make when fishing a spinner bait is to maintain a continuous retrieve that seldom allows the lure to work more than a few feet below the surface. The spinning blade tends to bring the lure up off the bottom. One way to compensate for this is to stop your retrieve and let the lure flutter to the bottom. Fish will often hit the lure on the way down, so be sure to watch your line for the slightest movement. When using this retrieve and drop method, stay with the single-blade models since the tandem blades do not flutter well. To work a spinner bait on the surface, just begin your retrieve before it hits the water and then keep cranking it in at a brisk pace.

ARTIFICIAL LURES AND TRIGGERING MECHANISM

Many anglers fail to realize the great difference in presentation that exists between fishing with live bait and fishing with artificial lures. Each of these techniques appeals to very different aspects of fish behavior.

When we are fishing live bait, we are trying to tempt or cajole the fish into taking the bait. We take time presenting the bait and try to make it look as natural as possible. At the same time the fish spends more time looking over our offering, smelling it, and sometimes rolling it around in its mouth. Any angler who has fished with minnows or crawlers for walleyes can attest to how fussy and cautious fish can be in taking live bait.

The purpose of an artificial lure, however, is to provoke a strike. In contrast to live bait, most lures are retrieved quickly and the fish has only an instant to react. The response is almost like a reflex action. The fish doesn't investigate; it simply sees or hears something in its general vicinity and either attacks or lets it go by. We understand very little about why the attack response occurs. We do know that what triggers it one day may not work the next, or for that matter, may not work the next hour. We also know that certain aspects of lure presentation are the key to that triggering mechanism.

As we mentioned earlier in the chapter, the most important part of fishing is putting your lure at the right depth. But there is something in the speed, action, color, and size of the lure that triggers the attack response in a particular fish at a particular time. Thus it is important to vary your presentation at any given depth.

Speed

The speed of a retrieve is probably the most important of the triggering stimuli, but it is one that is seldom considered by many anglers. We have fished with hundreds of anglers, and the one manual skill that separates the experienced angler from the novice is how he retrieves his lure. We have watched some anglers spend hours casting the same lure and retrieving it at the same speed. The experienced angler tries a lure at two or three different speeds before giving up and changing lures. At an early age, Chet Meyers became aware of how important speed control can be.

"My father and I were fishing for northerns in the French River area of central Ontario. We had been casting large shallow-diving lures for over three hours without any luck.

I was only fourteen years old and had not yet developed my father's patience. Finally, I announced that I was fed up and was going to quit for the day. I reeled in my last cast as fast as possible, just to show Dad how irritated I was, when suddenly a five-pound northern climbed all over my lure. The reel handle spun wildly, bruising my knuckles, but I managed to hold on and land the fish. It didn't take long for Dad to put two and two together, and soon he was cranking his lure in even faster than I had done. For the next few minutes that pattern held, and the northerns launched vicious attacks on our fast-fleeing lures."

In such situations we cannot explain why speed triggers an attack, but maybe it is enough just to know that it may do so. At some times of the year, however, particularly the early spring and late fall, we do know why speed is a factor. As cold-blooded animals, fish move much slower when the water is colder. When the water temperature drops, the fish's metabolism slows down and so it does not attack a lure with as much vigor as it can in warm water. Don't expect a slow-moving bass in fifty-five degree water to hit a fast-moving lure—it just doesn't happen. So pay attention to water temperature. While fish have no control over their metabolism, we anglers can and should control the speed with which we retrieve lures.

Action

Most manufactured lures have a built-in action designed and tested by the people who sell them. Some lures have a tight, wobbling motion, and others have a more sweeping side-to-side motion. Often, the simple retrieve of a lure without any additional action by the angler triggers a strike. But at other times, what triggers a strike in a fish is a break in the normal action of the lure.

On a recent trip to Whiteshell Park in Manitoba, the staff of our In' Fisherman summer schools spent five days fishing exclusively for smallmouth bass. After trying a variety of lures at different depths, they established that one particular spinner, a Gladding Shyster, seemed to be the best producer when retrieved just off the bottom. For four days they all stayed with this lure because they were doing so well. But even with an established pattern, the type of action that the angler used became important. One of the guys caught two bass to every one that the others caught because he used a little snap of the rod tip every once in a while when reeling in his lure. He had discovered this trick on river smallmouth, and it just happened to work on these lake bass. Somehow, the abrupt break in the action of the lure triggered them into striking.

It is important for you to know the action of the lures in your tackle box, and we would like to make a suggestion that, however silly it may seem at first, can really open your eyes to lure movement. Practice retrieving a few of your lures in a deserted swimming pool. By retrieving them through the clear water, you can see how they perform. You can also experiment with different types of retrieves and observe how what you do with your rod influences their action. Try stopping the retrieve and then starting it again. It may surprise you to see how tantalizing a lure looks when it suddenly stops and begins to float to the surface. No one action, of course, will produce all the time, and we believe that if you try different types of retrieves, you are going to add a lot more fish to your stringer.

Color

Can fish distinguish color? This question has been debated for years, but now we have proof that they can. Their eyes have both rods and cones, and the cones help them to recognize different shades of colors. On certain occasions we have watched two anglers, both using the same lure, at the same depth with the same action, and one would catch fish while the other got skunked. The reason why was that their lures were of different colors. We don't want to over-emphasize this point because color is not always an important stimulus, but when it does trigger an attack, it can make all the difference in the world. When you locate actively feeding fish, it usually doesn't matter what you

Manipulate the speed of the retrieve, the action of the lure, and the choice of color to provoke a strike.

throw at them. When they are in a neutral mood, however, your choice of color becomes significant.

We suggest buying your favorite lure in at least two different colors. A light color and a dark color would be a good choice. Most anglers agree that it is best to fish light colors, like white or yellow, on bright days and to try dark colors on overcast days. Also be aware of colors that seem especially good on your favorite lake or river. On the Saint Croix River in Minnesota, yellow seems to be extremely effective. One of our friends who fishes there regularly has a little bottle of yellow enamel that he uses to touch up many lures that he can't buy in that color.

Size

Like color, size is not always a crucial variable. Action and speed are far more important, and yet there are times when size is a consideration. There is some truth to the saying, "big lure, big fish" in that oversize lures, like a muskie-size Jitterbug, usually intimidates smaller fish. There are many occasions, however, when tiny lures will catch real lunkers.

One point to consider when choosing between lures of different sizes is that the smaller models usually don't run quite as deep as the larger ones. Again, we would suggest choosing one type of lure and then getting a few different sizes. There will be times when a 5/8-ounce lure will work and others when a tiny 1/4-ounce lure will just kill them.

PLASTIC WORMS

No chapter on lures would be complete without mention of the plastic worm and the increasing variety of worm-type baits now on the market. The plastic worm comes in many shapes, sizes, colors, and even flavors. It has caught just about every game fish that swims, but it is most effective on largemouth bass. The debate over how to fish this lure properly has been raging for more than two decades and will probably never be settled. Some anglers insist that you must let the bass run with the worm and then set the hook. Others believe that you should strike as soon as you feel the telltale "tick" that indicates the bass has inhaled your offering. Ray Scott, president of Bass Anglers Sportsman Society (BASS), goes even further. He feels that anglers should strike just about a second or two before they feel the "tick" (figure that one out). Anglers also debate the use of different sinkers and how the hook should be imbedded in the worm.

Whatever way you decide to fish the plastic worm, keep this in mind—it is different from other artificial lures. When fishing the plastic worm, we treat it almost like live bait. We are seeking to tempt the fish into feeding, and we are

Plastic worms (top to bottom): Ringworm, Swipe Tail, Sintepede, Reaper.

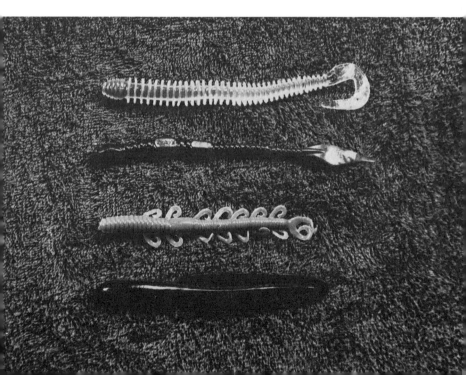

not relying on triggering an instinctive strike response. This means that a slow presentation is important. Plastic worm fishing takes time and patience. Casts must be accurate, and the retrieve is generally very slow. A crank bait or spinner bait angler can make five casts to every one of a worm angler. Still, there are times when nothing in the tackle box will outproduce the plastic worm.

One of the beauties of this lure is that when the tip of the hook is buried in the worm body, it becomes virtually weedless. On occasions when bass move into thick weeds or heavy timber, the plastic worm is hard to beat. It can also be an excellent choice when bass get "tight-lipped" after a cold front. If you haven't learned how to fish this lure, arrange an outing with a friend who knows how it is done. You won't be sorry.

HINTS FOR IMPROVEMENT

We hope that this chapter has helped you analyze your own fishing style as it pertains to artificial lures. The key consideration to keep in mind is fishing any given area at different depths. On page 127 is a chart that should help you analyze your own strengths and weaknesses regarding depth. By using this chart to analyze the lures that are presently in your tackle box and the amount of time you spend using each of these lures, you should be able to tell how versatile you really are.

After completing the chart, decide what type of lure you do not use that you would like to master. Select two or three lures of this type in different colors and sizes, and spend half a day on the water learning how to fish them. This will take real discipline. Most of us try a new lure for three or four casts and then go back to the old standbys. If it is possible, ask a friend to go along who knows the finer points of fishing this lure. Be sure to read the instructions that come with the lure. They will often tell you about different

Type of lure	Normal depth	Total number	Lure names and variety (i.e., red/white Daredevles)	How heavily do you rely on this type of lure?			
				Often	Avg.	Seldom	Not at all
Surface	Surface only						
Shallow divers (floating)	1-7 feet						
Deep divers (floating and sinking)	7-20 feet						
Spoons and spinners	Usually mid-depths and deep						
Jigs	Usually bottom						
Spinner baits	Surface, mid-depths, and deep						
Plastic worms	Usually bottom						

Angler versatility index: artificial lures.

types of retrieves and the normal depth that this lure will run. Even before making your first cast, hold the lure in the water next to the boat and work it back and forth so that you have some idea how it is supposed to work. Most lures must be tied directly to the line without any snaps or swivels, but a snap may even enhance the action of others.

Once you start using the lure, concentrate on feeling its action through your rod tip. Get used to feeling what it is like when the lure is working properly. You can usually tell when a lure picks up weeds, and even the smallest amount of weeds kills the action of most lures. When trying out your new lure, experiment with different speeds and types of retrieves. Above all, don't give up simply because the lure doesn't work miracles the first time you use it. Try to imagine circumstances when it would be really appropriate and experiment with it then. Most likely, it will soon become a working member of your tackle box.

It is generally foolish to make any promises when talking about fishing, but we promise that if you can master a few lures in each of the categories we have outlined and if you try different speeds, actions, colors, and sizes, you are going to catch a lot more fish than before. Our theme throughout this book has been that versatility is the key to successful fishing, and knowing how to use a variety of lures is one of the most important aspects of angler versatility.

chapter 8

From Suckers to Sallies

It was mid-July, one of the few times that it gets really hot in Minnesota. The temperature had been hovering in the high eighties for the past week, and the humidity was almost unbearable. The bass fishing was pretty good on local lakes, but the real challenge lay in trying to dredge up some lunker northerns. One steamy afternoon at the In' Fisherman office, we were talking about these "toothy critters" and plotting a variety of tactics. Despite their voracious appetite and their often-alleged stupidity, northerns that weigh over ten pounds are hard to come by. In fact, big northerns can be the toughest of all game fish to catch during the summer. We debated various approaches until Ron Lindner exclaimed, "There's no doubt about it. If I were to fish for big northerns right now, I'd stick a big sucker minnow on a hook, slip on a bobber, find some likely point near deep water, and just wait them out."

It may come as a shock to some anglers that with all the sophisticated tackle and equipment on the market, there is still a time and place for bobber fishing with live bait. Many anglers feel it is somehow beneath them or that they are taking unfair advantage of the fish by using live bait. This

Sometimes, using live bait is the only way to entice lunker northerns to open their jaws.

is untrue. In many ways, the selection and presentation of live bait takes more skill than the use of artificial lures. When fishing with artificials, we are relying on triggering an instinctive strike from the fish. The fish sees the lure for a very short period of time, strikes quickly out of instinct, and often hooks itself. Using live bait is a very different matter. Fish use their microscopic vision to look it over carefully before deciding, and a sloppily baited hook or a bait that is presented unnaturally is usually ignored.

The skills involved in fishing live bait focus on presenting the bait in the most natural way possible so that it looks as if it is free swimming. If you doubt this, try a little experiment. Get some small angleworms and take them down to a boat dock where you know there are some sunfish or small bass. Drop a few in the water. Watch how naturally they wiggle as they fall toward the bottom and see how quickly they get snapped up by the fish. Now take one of the worms and put it on a medium-size hook, the kind you usually use, and lower it into the water. The fish will approach cautiously. It may smell and look like a worm, but they can tell just by the way it falls through the water that there is something different about it. No, live bait fishing isn't easy, nor is it taking unfair advantage of the fish.

Every angler should know at least two or three techniques for fishing live bait. Over the centuries innumerable ways have been developed—some as simple as a safety pin on a string and some so complicated that it would take an engineer to figure them out. You probably have your own favorite techniques. Here are three that we guarantee will produce fish.

SLIP SINKERS: THE WALLEYE FISHERMAN'S DREAM COME TRUE

The slip sinker is not a new development in fishing, but it has really become popular only in the last ten years. River fishermen have been using this type of rig for thirty or forty years. As with other fishing techniques, however, it often takes a major breakthrough to make them popular with the majority of anglers.

The slip sinker in its simplest form is nothing more than a piece of lead with a hole through the center. The line is fed through the hole, and a hook is tied to the end of the line. Then a stopper of some sort is affixed about twenty inches or so above the hook to prevent it from sliding through the hole. The advantage of this arrangement over the regular stationary sinker is that when the fish takes the bait, it can move off freely without dragging the heavy sinker around. River anglers adopted this method because there was often a need for a heavy weight to keep the bait on the bottom in a fast current. They rigged their line with an egg-shaped sinker, and when they felt a bite, they released the line to let the fish swallow the bait without feeling the sinker.

Lake fishermen did not start using this method until some Midwest anglers began experimenting with it as a trolling technique for walleyes. The principle was exactly the same. With a moving boat it was necessary to have enough weight to keep the bait near the bottom and yet allow it to run free at the slightest tap from a fish. The egg sinker kept the bait near the bottom, but it had a tendency to hang up quite easily. It wasn't until the development of the walking sinker that fishing with slip sinkers caught on with most walleye anglers.

The peculiar shape of the walking sinker allows it to bounce along the bottom and "walk" over rocks, logs, and other tiresome snags. The present model is the result of modifications by many anglers, but Bill Binkleman, a Wisconsin angler and tackle manufacturer, really helped to make this rig popular. Ron Lindner made some additional modifications, and now the walking slip sinker is found from one end of the country to the other.

This rig is particularly effective, not only because it keeps you in the fish-catching zone, but also because you can use light line and small hooks, which are two important elements when seeking a fish as wary as the walleye. One day Al and Ron Lindner were out on Gull Lake, slowly back trolling a drop-off area that consistently produced walleyes. They were experimenting with slip sinkers of different weights as well as various baits. At first they relied heavily on night crawlers and minnows, but they soon found leeches to be terrific producers.

"The fishing had been tough the last few days, and the fish weren't coming too fast. We knew that the smaller the hook, the more natural the crawler would appear to the walleye. On this particular day we were amazed how much

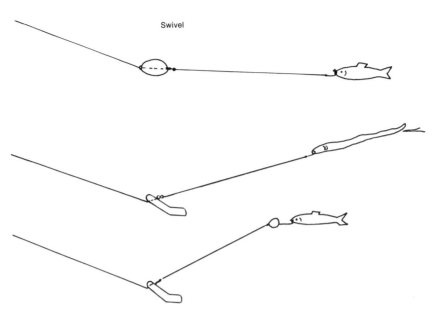

Swivel

Slip sinker rigs (from top to bottom): the old, egg-type sinker; the walking sinker with an air-injected crawler; the walking sinker with a floating jig. Slip sinkers are an excellent way to fish live bait because they keep the bait near the bottom. If you want to keep the bait a little bit above the bottom, inject a crawler with air, or use a floating jig and minnow combination.

difference both the hook size and the line weight made. Ron was outfishing me about three-to-one simply because he had gone to six-pound test. While most anglers seldom use smaller than a size 6 hook, we were both using size 8. But even with a small hook, the diameter of the line is crucial. When walleyes get picky they can be real tough, so I decided to go even lighter and switched to four-pound test and a size 10 hook. It wasn't long before I was outproducing Ron. There have been some instances, believe it or not, when we have had to go as light as two-pound test before catching fish."

It's important when fishing this rig to keep it close to the bottom. You should feel it tick the bottom every once in a while just to make sure you are down in the fish-catching zone. Back trolling, a technique that we mentioned briefly in chapter 4, is one of the best ways to use any bait with a slip sinker for walleyes.

To back troll, just put your motor in reverse and back your boat stern-first in the direction you intend to go. This technique has a number of advantages. First, it helps slow the boat down so that your sinker and bait can reach the bottom. It doesn't take much speed to lift a bait four or five feet off the bottom, and if you are that far away from the bottom, you are probably missing most of the fish. The second advantage is that back trolling gives you much greater boat control, particularly in a wind. When you troll forward, the wind can push the bow of the boat around and move you away from structure and concentrations of fish. By using a depth finder and by back trolling, you can stay

When back trolling, three anglers can fish out of one boat easily without tangling their lines.

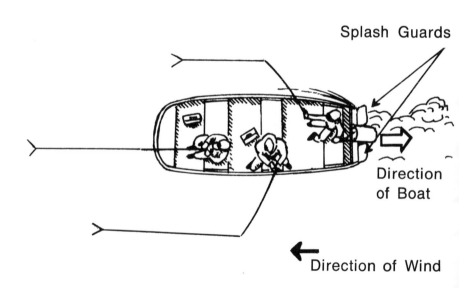

right on the edge of weed beds or drop-offs. A third advantage is that three people can troll out of one boat with a
minimum of confusion. The person in the stern can fish
on the left side, the one in the middle can fish on the right
side, and the person in the bow can work straight out.
Lines do not get tangled, and there is no danger of getting
lines caught under the motor once a fish is hooked. Whenever a "pickup" is felt, the motor can be slipped into neutral
and the fish given enough slack line before setting the hook.
If all goes well, the other anglers need not even reel in their
lines.

Once fish are located, it helps to throw out a marker
buoy so that you can return to the area on your next pass.
Marker buoys can be purchased or made out of old Clorox
bottles. You should always recheck any area where you
pick up a fish, since there very well may be a school there
that could make for some fast action.

Though back trolling is much slower than other forms of
trolling, it is perhaps one of the most effective means of
locating fish. Once fish are located, be sure to note the
speed and direction of your movement. On numerous occasions we have pinpointed a school of walleyes or bass and
found that the direction of our approach was crucial. We
would pass over our spot from one direction and pick up
one or two fish. Then we would swing around and go over
the same spot and get nothing. The next pass would be
made in the direction of the original contact, and again
we would get fish.

The normal equipment for back trolling includes an
open face reel and line no heavier than eight-pound test. A
size 8 hook is standard, and the weight of the sinker depends on the depth of the water and the speed of the boat.
We always keep the bail of our reel open and pin the line
to the rod with one finger. Often, the "pickup" feels like
only a small tap on the line, but the size of the tap is no

indication of the size of the fish. Some of the biggest wall-eyes we've taken have barely touched the bait. When the tap is felt, all you need to do is to release your finger and the line runs freely.

There are no hard-and-fast rules about how long you should wait before setting the hook. The best approach is to let the fish have it for only a few seconds. Then, slowly reel up and set the hook firmly. Be sure to pick up all the slack line before setting the hook. With the time the fish has had to take out line, it could have run in any direction, even back toward you. If you try to set the hook against twenty feet of slack line, you are bound to miss the fish. If you miss the first fish even after getting rid of the slack, wait a little longer before setting the hook the next time. Walleyes can be very finicky, and sometimes they need twenty seconds or more to swallow the bait.

Though back trolling is the predominant way in which slip sinkers are used, they work very well when still-fished or even cast. When casting one of these rigs, however, care must be taken not to tear the bait off the hook during the cast. The normal overhand cast is too quick, and the snap of the rod can tear off crawlers and minnows. It is better to use a gentle sidearm cast. Some anglers who still-fish in rivers put a small clip on the end of the rod so that they can keep their bail open and yet prevent the line from tumbling downstream a long distance. The clip serves a function like that of an outrigger on a deep-sea fishing boat. When the fish takes the bait, the line pulls free from the clip and the angler knows he has a fish.

TRICKS AND TIPS

After Al Lindner started fishing with slip sinkers, he experimented with a variety of adaptations. One of them, in particular, is a little startling at first glance.

" 'Hey! What are you doing to that crawler?' asked my

boat partner one day when he spied me shooting a little air into the tail of my bait with a hypodermic needle. 'Nothing,' I replied and hoped he wouldn't press me for an explanation. I had picked this tip up in a conversation with another angler, and I wanted to try it alongside someone fishing with a nonaerated worm to see if it made any difference. The air lifts the crawler off the bottom, whereas without the air the worm drags across the bottom. Unless fish are in an extremely negative mood, they are usually a foot or so off the bottom. My hope was that the air would put my crawler right next to their mouths.

" 'I've got a pickup,' I said, as I slipped the boat into neutral. I slowly reeled up and set the hook into a nice three-pound walleye. Luckily, the stringer was in the bow of the boat, and while my buddy was stringing the fish, I quickly pumped up another crawler.

On our next pass I was into another fish. Now my friend was no dummy, and this time he turned toward me to watch as he strung the fish. I figured, 'What the hell,' and made no attempt to conceal what I was doing. He looked on in disbelief.

" 'What are you putting in that thing—joy juice?'

" 'No, just air. Here, you try it this time, and I'll go with a straight crawler,' I said, tossing him the air-injected worm. The tip was a good one because on the next pass, my friend was leaning into four pounds of walleye and I was netting the fish."

The problem with early attempts at pumping up worms was that the needle kept getting clogged. This nuisance has since been avoided by using larger-gauge needles, and now most sport stores sell cheap squeeze bottles with a short needle for this purpose.

Another ingenious modification of the slip sinker rig was again the result of Bill Binkleman's pioneering work. Bill began experimenting with cork jigs as a means of keeping

Bill Binkleman, flanked by Al and Ron Lindner, with a nice string of cold water walleyes taken on floating jigs.

bait well off the bottom. By painstakingly slicing tiny cork balls in half and then gluing them together on the eye end of a hook, Bill got what he wanted. He tried a variety of colors and soon hit on fluorescents as a real fish attractor. The cork jig was a major breakthrough because while crawlers could be air injected, minnows could not. The cork jig is still a recent development and has only begun to spread across the country. Bill insists that the fluorescent colors excite the fish so that they strike at the bait rather than gently sucking it in as they normally do. We're not sure what the fluorescent cork jig does to the fish, but we do know that it works and that during cold water periods it will outproduce just about any other technique for catching walleyes.

FISHING THE WATER DRAGON

Anglers are a stubborn breed, and old habits are hard to change. Al Lindner had heard rumors of bass fishermen in the Far West using salamanders as long as forty years ago, but somehow this method never made it to the Midwest. In Florida, expert bass anglers have also been using a variety of salamander called a siren for decades, but once again the technique never moved out of the state. And it took a while for Al to try out the "water dragon," too.

" 'What the heck do you have in that styrofoam box?' I asked as we pushed off from the dock. The man in the bow of the boat just smiled and said, 'Salamanders.' The time was June 1968. The place was Whitefish Lake in Minnesota. And the man with the salamanders was Carl Lowrance, inventor of the magic box that revolutionized fishing, the Lowrance depth finder. Carl had flown these creatures all the way from his home in Tulsa, Oklahoma, just to convince us that he had discovered a new technique for big walleyes. Carl assured us that he had caught walleyes in the eight-to-ten-pound category on salamanders. I had heard of using waterdogs, a type of salamander, for muskies, but I was unaware of their potential as big walleye bait.

"The problem with this day was that the salamanders never got a fair trial. We were out trying to film some footage for a TV show, and with the pressure to produce fish for the cameraman, we didn't want to waste too much time experimenting. Besides, the walleyes were just tearing up the leeches and crawlers that we offered them, and none of us was too excited about changing bait. Every once in a while someone would halfheartedly put a salamander on a live bait rig and drag it around the lake and then watch as the others hauled in the walleyes. Soon Carl had on a crawler, too, and when he banged into a nine-pound walleye, that just about settled the matter. The 'sallies' stayed in the bait box for the remainder of the trip.

"For the next six years the salamander project stayed on the back burner. We probably would have forgotten about it altogether were it not for Dick Burnelle. Dick runs a bait business in the Brainerd area, which Ron, my brother, and I use almost exclusively. Dick kept coming up with salamanders in his minnow traps and asked Ron and me about the possibility of using them for bait. We remembered our earlier experience and vowed to give it one more try. The next time we stopped in for some bait, Dick had a bunch of six-to-nine-inch salamanders waiting for us. It was early in the fall of 1974, and the fishing on Gull Lake had been less than fantastic, so we decided that we didn't have much to lose. We tossed some salamanders into a large bait bucket and headed out for lunker walleyes.

"When you are used to hooking a crawler or small leech on a size 8 hook for walleyes, the prospect of hooking an eight-inch salamander on a substantially larger hook seems a little ludicrous. We selected a bay that had produced big walleyes in the past and slowly lowered our water dragons over the side of the boat. Ron and I started chatting about a new fishing magazine that we were working on and weren't paying much attention, when something slammed into Rod's salamander and nearly tore the rod from his grip. Quickly, Ron played out line to the speeding fish, but when he reeled in and set the hook, the fish was gone. The salamander was dead as a doornail and badly mangled. We looked it over carefully but couldn't tell if its attacker had been a northern or a walleye. The strike spelled northern to me. A few minutes later, the same thing happened to me. Now I just knew it was a northern. No walleye I'd ever run into had hit like that. I reeled up to set the hook, but the fish was gone. Once again, the salamander came in looking as if it had been through a meat grinder. This was embarassing. Even if these were northerns, we were determined to hang a couple of them.

"I rigged up again, and we started trolling by the area that had brought us our last two strikes—nothing happened. As I turned the boat for another pass, my rod almost jumped out of the boat. This time, I didn't wait as long to set the hook, and when I did, I hit pay dirt. 'Well, we finally got one, and it's no hammer handle. This is a nice northern.' But even as I spoke, the pumping on the end of my line told me I was wrong. I slugged it out toe-to-toe, and when Ron scooped up the fish, the net sagged with an eight-pound walleye.

"On the next pass it was Ron's turn. I figure that brothers should always take turns, and that's exactly what we were doing. The walleye struck in the same uncharacteristic manner, hitting like a freight train and peeling off line at an amazing rate. This one was slightly bigger and just

All caught on salamanders.

topped 9 pounds. It was too good to be true. There was a brief lull in the action and then another savage strike. This time it was only a baby walleye, running about 7½ pounds. We now had three fish that weighed more than 25 pounds! We were both ecstatic, but I couldn't help thinking about the six years that we had kept this project in the back of our minds."

Since that day on Gull Lake we have tried salamanders on walleyes, largemouth, smallmouth, northerns, and muskie. They work extremely well on almost all game fish and can be used spring, summer, and fall. The biggest problem is their unavailability through bait stores. At present, few stores stock them regularly, and those that do, carry them in the six- to nine-inch category. For this reason, their use is limited to big fish—you don't pick up too many small fish on an eight-inch bait!

CATCHING YOUR OWN SALLIES

North America is amply blessed with close to half of the three-hundred-odd species of salamanders known to science. They range in size from the 1½-inch pigmy salamander to hellbenders that exceed 20 inches and sirens that can reach a length of 3 feet or more. The salamanders that we use range in size from 5 to 10 inches. The most common variety in the eastern United States and the Midwest is the tiger salamander. Another common variety is the red spotted newt. In its adult stage the tiger salamander is air breathing, so when fishing it, be sure to bring it up for air. Immature tiger salamanders, however, have external gills that are easily visible, and they can be kept underwater indefinitely.

Hunting salamanders may take you back to your childhood days, and there is a serious possibility that you will get so wrapped up in the search for bait that you'll forget the lunker fish you are really after. The best time of the year to look for sallies is early spring when they migrate to their breeding areas near woodland pools. Even many of the varieties that live on land lay their eggs in the water. Go prepared with rubber boots, a small net or scoop, and a bait bucket. Keep the bucket filled with moss or leaves and an inch or two of water. Make sure it has a snap-down lid, since salamanders can easily crawl up the sides of most containers.

Look for salamanders under piles of damp leaves and inside hollow logs near pools and streams. Rotting logs are one of their prime habitats, and one log may yield several sallies. Small streams also attract these creatures, and they can often be found by turning over rocks on stream bottoms or near the edge of the water.

Salamanders can be kept alive at home in the garage in a steep-sided, screen-covered container. They need a combination of water and dry land. A large metal tub works well, since it can be filled with a few inches of water and then some rocks or logs can be placed at one end so the salamanders can come out of the water to breathe. They eat just about anything. We usually feed ours dead minnows, but worms or hamburger also work. Make sure to keep them well fed because if you don't, they will begin eating each other. Remove any dead ones and change the water regularly, so they don't eat decomposed food and become diseased.

HOW TO RIG SALAMANDERS FOR LUNKER FISH

We have found that the best way to fish salamanders is on a slip sinker rig. The weight of the sinker depends on the size of the salamander and the boat speed. Slow back trolling is the best approach. Choose a lake that has big fish and be prepared to wait for a while. It may be a long time before your first strike.

Salamanders are best fished over a clean bottom or near the edge of the weedline. They are very difficult to still-fish or to fish in weeds because they have a natural tendency to hide under rocks or in the weeds and are likely to get hung up. If you are going to fish them, be prepared to keep moving. While the slip sinker is the best all-around technique, there are times in the early spring when they can be fished with a large split shot about two feet ahead of the hook. This rig is particularly deadly for northerns and muskies before the weeds come up in their shallow spawning bays. We call it free lining or flat lining. Simply clamp on a split shot, hook up your sallie, let out forty feet of line, and slowly move around the bay with a trolling motor. Then hang on tight. Not many northerns can resist the sight of a lazy old salamander swimming along in their bay.

When you get your first hit on a salamander, you won't soon forget it. While most big fish gently suck in live bait such as worms, leeches, and minnows, they usually hit a sallie with a vicious, jolting strike. We are not sure of the reason for this ferocious attack, but it could be an instinctive reaction. Some aquatic species of salamander, like mud puppies and hellbenders, feed on fish eggs and young fry. It's possible that these adult fish are trying to kill a predator that feeds on their young. We found that we missed a lot of our first fish because we waited too long to set the hook. After the initial run, a fish would often spit out the dead sallie. This leads us to believe that the fish are simply trying to kill the salamander and are not interested in eating it. Another reason for spitting out the bait might be that some salamanders have a toxic slime covering their body that protects them from being eaten by predators.

Whatever the reason for this hit-and-run tactic, we modified our original single-hook rigging by attaching a treble hook near the tail of the sallie so that we could strike immediately with a good chance of hooking the fish.

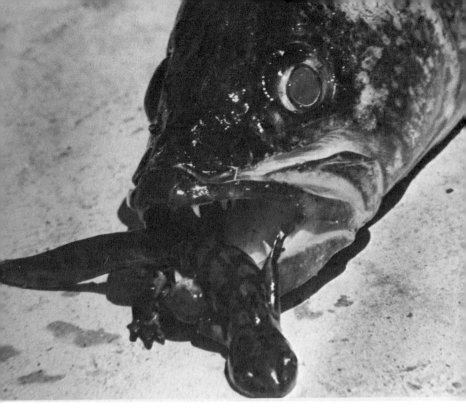
The water dragon and an eight-pound victim.

While they are good bait throughout the year, salamanders are especially effective during the cold water spring and fall periods. Whatever time of year you decide to try them, don't expect immediate action. It may take some time before you locate big fish, but when you do, there will be no doubt about it.

THE BEST ALL-AROUND COMBINATION
IN THE WORLD

The jig and minnow combination is without a doubt the most successful marriage of live bait and artificial bait in existence. If we had to choose one technique to use in any part of the country—from the Finger Lakes of New York to the reservoirs of California—it would be the jig and minnow. This combination works well on almost every species of game fish during all times of the year in almost any body of water. That's quite a recommendation.

The jig and minnow is most effective during the early spring before and after the spawn, and it works well going into the summer months. During the summer there are times when other methods, like the slip sinker, can be more productive, but the jig and minnow will still catch fish. It can be fished in the early fall and is dynamite in the cold water period just before the freeze on northern lakes. It is even a good technique through the ice.

The reason for the success of this combination is threefold. First, you don't have to be a skilled angler to use it. Fish are attracted to both the action of the jig and the smell of live bait. And since novice anglers often have their most difficult time learning to set the hook quickly and properly, the presence of live bait buys a little time. While fish reject most artificials very quickly, they hang on a little longer because of the presence of the minnow. The second advantage is that the jig, because of its weight, keeps the minnow near the bottom, which is most often the fish-catching zone. Finally, the action that can be imparted to jigs is limited only by the imagination of the angler. Jigs can appear to swim in a side-to-side motion, or they can jump or crawl slowly across the bottom. They can even be still-fished right on the bottom. Thus, without changing lures, you can present your jig and minnow in a variety of styles in order to trigger the fish to action.

Despite all these advantages, it is surprising how little known the jig and minnow combination is outside the north central United States. In our travels to other parts of the country, we have met few anglers who have adapted this deadly combination to their own lakes and rivers. Even the guides of northern Canada, who host fishermen from all over the world and who often rely on plain jigs as lures, do not use a jig and minnow in combination. Southern anglers have for years relied on a jig head with a plastic worm or eel as a popular rig for bass. They could use the same weedless jig heads, attach a minnow, and knock the bass dead, particularly in the cold winter months when things slow down a bit. Bass are bass and walleyes are walleyes no matter where you find them, and we have proved the effectiveness of this technique across the country. We are convinced that when anglers elsewhere in Canada and the United States adopt the jig and minnow combination, they will double or triple their catches.

YOUR CHOICE OF JIGS AND MINNOWS

We touched briefly on types of jigs in the last chapter. The type that you select will depend on the lake or river conditions that you encounter. Since we often like to fish the edge of weedlines for bass, northerns, and walleyes, we prefer a spearhead type of jig. The shape of the head lets the jig drop easily through the weeds, and it does not hang up. The weight depends on the depth of the water, but usually a 1/4 or 3/8 ounce works well. In rivers we especially like Dan Gapen's Ugly Bug. The shape of the head helps keep the jig down in a current, and the offset eyelet prevents it from hanging up. One day last summer, Chet caught over forty walleyes and smallmouth on the same Ugly Bug while fishing a rocky section of the Mississippi. The plain ball type of jig works well on clean bottoms and is popular in many sections of the country.

The dressing that is on the jig can also have a great deal to do with its effectiveness. Dressings include bucktail, feathers, plastic twister worms, and grubs. You will discover what works best for you under specific conditions, but for cold water fishing, be sure to get some jigs with maribou feathers. The maribou moves tantalizingly in the water with no current at all. It is a fantastic jig dressing to use on walleyes or bass when the cold water makes them sluggish.

A variety of minnows can be used with the jig, but the hardiest are obviously the most effective. Fatheads and sucker minnows are available in most parts of the country and are probably the best. They have amazing endurance and can stay on the hook through thick and thin. Although shiners are excellent bait, they are hard to keep alive and just don't last as long as fatheads.

HOW TO STRIKE BEFORE THE HIT

Time and time again, divers have confirmed that fish almost always take a lure or bait while it is dropping. To the angler, this means a lot of missed fish, because when a jig is dropping, there is usually slack in the line. Thus he does not feel the take, and by the time he is aware of it, the fish has spit out the jig. By forgetting about your sense of feel and by using your sense of sight, however, you can easily double the number of fish you catch when using a jig. It's a trick that Chet Meyers has been using for years, and he'll never forget the first time he tried it.

"I was on the Saint Croix and had missed a number of bass while fishing a yellow bucktail jig and fathead minnow. They would just grab and let go. I recalled an article I had read and remembered that the author said to strike *before* you felt the hit. He maintained that by watching the line as the jig is dropping in the water, you could almost always tell if a fish had hit your jig. Either the line would stop dropping before it hit bottom, or you would see it jerk off to one side. Well, having missed the last six smallmouth that grabbed at my jig, I didn't have much to lose.

"On the fourth cast it happened. As the line dropped, it suddenly made a small twitch to one side. So, I did what the man said—I struck. It was a strange sensation, almost like striking into thin air. I was sure that the jig would fly back and hit me in the face, but instead I hit a two-pound smallmouth in the face. The next hit was a little different.

I knew I was fishing in more than ten feet of water, but the line stopped dropping after only the first foot or so. There was no twitch in the line this time; the line just stopped as if it were suspended seven feet off the bottom. It was. It was suspended in another smallie's mouth. Once again I struck, without ever feeling a tug from the fish. At the end of the day I had four smallmouth and two white bass, all of which I might not have known were there had it not been for the unfelt signals that my line sent back to me. Since that day on the river I would say that my success ratio while jig fishing has improved 40 percent."

To use this technique, you need high visibility line; that is, a line that picks up the sun's rays above water and yet is not visible to the fish below. Fluorescent Blue Stren is a good line for this purpose. It's difficult to go against all common sense and past experience to set the hook before you feel the fish, but we suggest you try it.

RIGGING THE MINNOW

The best approach for a jig and minnow is to tie the jig directly to your line without any swivel or snap. Be sure to check the knot every once in a while since continual casting will weaken it, but do not use snaps or swivels. They will only detract from your presentation. Walleyes and bass will not bite through your line, and you will be surprised how many northerns you can land without a leader.

A trick that is particularly effective when using large minnows for bait is to add a stinger hook to your jig, similar to the one we worked out for the salamander rig. This is simply a treble hook that is attached by a piece of wire or monofilament to the back hook. Hook the main hook of the jig up through the lower jaw of the minnow and stick one of the treble hooks into the rear end of the minnow. This is a technique that works well during periods of cold water when fish are less likely to attack and swallow

The addition of a stinger hook to a jig works well on short-striking fish and is particularly deadly during the spring and fall when the water is cold.

the minnow whole. We find it a particularly good technique to use with sucker minnows in the five- to eight-inch category. If you are going to use it on northerns or muskies, use wire leader or at least twenty-pound monofilament.

LEARNING FROM OTHER REGIONS

As we travel the country, we are constantly learning new techniques. The three live bait methods outlined in this chapter have been used in different regions for the last decade, but for the most part they have remained in those regions. Most anglers are more than happy to share their techniques with others, but for some, this sharing never progresses beyond the talking stage. And yet the true mark of a successful angler is experimentation. If it works on Canadian smallmouth, why won't it work on Kentucky bass? Maybe the technique they use on lake trout in New York can be applied to walleyes in Tennessee. Those are interesting speculations, but the only way you will find the answer is to give it a try. Go ahead. You've got nothing to lose but some fishing time, and who knows what you have to gain—maybe the lunker of a lifetime!

chapter 9

The Confident Angler

In early April, when fishermen in the South are already catching crappies, white bass, and fat, spawning largemouths, most lakes in the upper Midwest still have a foot of ice on them. The fishing season is still six weeks away, but the fishing and camping show draws thousands of frustrated anglers to downtown Minneapolis. Al Lindner often attends these shows, making presentations on the only subject that is nearer and dearer to the hearts of Minnesotans than the Vikings—spring walleye fishing. He has this story to tell about one knowledgeable angler he met there.

"It was at last year's show that I first met Ray Brown. He pulled me aside after my talk and offered to buy me lunch. Ray said that he had a few questions about walleyes that I hadn't covered, and since I had the next two hours free, I agreed to join him. As we talked, it became clear to me that here was a guy who really knew a lot about walleyes. He had read just about everything that had been written about 'old marbleyes' and knew the fish backwards and forwards. As we parted company, he thanked me for taking the time and said he would like to stop by my office someday when he was passing through the Brainerd area.

"Two months later Ray called to ask if we could get together for a morning of fishing, and soon we were out on the water, headed for one of my favorite weed beds. With all Ray's knowledge, I was confident that we would do well, in spite of the fact that the lake I had chosen was a tough one to fish. The weather had been calm, and I was pretty sure we could pick up some walleyes by working some thick weed beds near deep water.

"When we reached the edge of the weed bed, I rigged with a jig and minnow and began casting just into the weeds. Ray spent some time looking through his tackle box and then asked what I was using. I tossed him a spearhead jig and told him how to rig a red-tailed chub properly. Fishing was slow, but by moving around I managed to land three walleyes in the two-pound category during the first two hours of fishing. Ray had nothing, and his earlier enthusiasm had slipped away. He fell silent and began changing lures to see what else might work. Nothing seemed to help. The fishing got tougher, and by the time we headed in at noon, we had landed only two more fish—I got both of them. During the morning I had recognized something I have seen time and time again with other fishing partners. Here was a guy who knew more about walleyes than 99 percent of the anglers I had ever met, and yet he couldn't catch them. Ray was the classic case of an angler who lacked confidence, and I am convinced that this was the reason he got 'skunked.' "

While knowledge of fish habits and habitat is crucial to being a versatile and successful angler, it is not enough in itself. You must also believe in your ability to catch fish. When you fish with confidence, you just know that you are going to catch fish. As soon as you get to the lake, you start planning your tactics and where you are going to use them. When you motor past a certain spot, a weed bed in ten feet of water, for instance, you know the bass are there.

Finally landing a lunker like this is the result of hard work, a lot of confidence, and very little luck.

You know that you are going to catch them and that a spinner bait with a white skirt will do the trick. It may seem crazy, but when you have confidence, that's how it is.

If you don't have confidence, you probably know that, too. One symptom of a lack of confidence is that lost feeling many anglers get when they approach a new body of water. Their heads swim with questions such as "Where are the fish?" and "What will I use?" Even before the first cast, they are having serious doubts that they will even see a fish. They might select one spot and start casting, but soon they really aren't paying attention to what they are doing. Instead, they are worried about getting skunked, and under these circumstances, they usually are.

Confidence is an intangible, and it is something quite apart from expertise. Reading every book or magazine article written about your favorite game fish and attending every fishing clinic that comes your way will not help you build confidence. Confidence comes only from time on the water and trial and error. It is certainly born of success, but it is not deterred by occasional failure. It comes from mastering a few techniques on a familiar lake so that, over a period of time, you prove to yourself that you can catch fish under a variety of circumstances.

FRED'S MAGIC FROGS

Perhaps one of the most important aspects of confidence is believing in the baits and lures that you use. Most of us have one or two favorite lures with which we have caught fish, and learning to use them properly under different conditions is an excellent way to begin building confidence. Chet Meyers has a fishing buddy who is a living example of what faith in your lures and baits can do.

"I'm not sure that my friend Fred ever read the fairy story of the Princess and the Frog, but I do know that he has an almost magical belief in frogs as bass bait. Fred's folks have a cabin on a small lake where I have fished with him on a number of occasions. Besides being fishing buddies, we are also good friends, and we abide by each other's methods whenever one of us is on the other's turf. When you fish on Fred's lake, you fish with frogs. There are a couple of bays that are favorites, and as we silently row around in those bays, our approach is always the same. We cast live frogs on weedless hook into the open pockets in the lily pads and wait for Mr. Bass.

"Fred usually outfishes me about three to one on frogs, and I am convinced that the main reason is that he just knows they are going to produce. I keep telling him that we should take another approach or even go for some of the lunker walleyes known to be in the lake, but Fred has eyes only for bass. He expects a fish on every cast, and so he is always ready for the strike. Put Fred on a river and his eyes glaze, but in a shallow bay when he's fishing with frogs, he's deadly."

Learning to work one or two baits or lures really well is the first step in gaining confidence. Look at one of your favorite lures. At what depth does it run? Under what conditions does it usually produce fish? Are there ways you can modify it to make it more effective? After you can answer these questions, work that lure until it almost becomes an extension of your arm and rod. One lure that you can have confidence in and can use under a variety of circumstances is worth ten of those that you don't believe in and don't know how to use properly.

The reason for this is really very simple. If you believe that a lure will produce, you are going to pay more attention when fishing it and you will fish it better. A big part of confidence is anticipation. When Al is working a tournament, for example, he is always poised and ready for the strike. He knows what his lure is doing when it is coming through the water, and he can feel even the slightest break

A big part of confidence is anticipating a strike on every cast.

in the action that might indicate a fish. Whenever he feels something unnatural, he strikes. Confident anglers make their own luck happen.

Most anglers who have confidence in a lure experiment with it and make minor changes, like fine tuning an engine. Spinner bait anglers like to use a pair of pliers to bend the blades of their lures to produce different vibrations. Jig fishermen design their own jig heads and produce some really strange-looking lures. River anglers who fish with live bait are probably the most innovative of all, but each of these experimenters shares one thing with the others: faith in his approach and the certainty that he will catch fish with it.

One of our friends loves to fish Rapalas for smallmouth bass in rivers. He has also caught a lot of bass on yellow jigs, and one day he put two and two together. Realizing that yellow was a super color for smallmouth, he bought some bright yellow enamel at a hobby store and doctored up a few Rapalas. At that time the lure came only in a silver or gold finish. After that he swore that he had the magical lure for river smallmouth. A few months later, he made another modification. He pinched the soft balsa wood Rapalas just slightly in the middle with a pair of longnose pliers. This made them run a little crooked and, according to him, drove the bass crazy.

The best place to start building confidence in your lures and baits is that lake or river that you chose according to the guidelines in chapter 5. Make sure that the lure you select is appropriate for the species you are after. The more versatile a lure is, the better. You may have confidence in a lure that works only under certain circumstances, as many surface plugs do. Fine, but when the conditions aren't right, don't stay with that lure. Besides, once you have confidence in a lure and know when it will and when it will not produce, it's time to move on to another lure. In this way you will build your versatility. If you want to learn how to use a new lure, fish with someone who already has confidence in such a lure and let him show you how to get started.

RECOGNIZING LOCATIONAL PATTERNS

A second and equally important aspect of confidence is the ability to recognize situations that have produced fish in the past. A friend of ours grew up fishing wing dams on rivers and as a consequence, fished rivers for years before he ever ventured out on a lake. While wing dams may vary greatly in size and composition, some basic principles will apply to most circumstances. Our buddy was an expert river angler, and wing dams were his specialty. Each time he fished them, he could predict with an uncanny ability the location and feeding mood of the fish: he had identified their locational pattern. He is now a good lake angler, but put him on a river in sight of a wing dam, and it's like old home week. He just knows he is going to catch fish.

Lake anglers learn to recognize other situations, such as types of weed beds and the shapes of bars and sunken islands. Once they identify a locational pattern, they often find that the same structure will produce fish on similar lakes. Locating a thick weed bed of a type we call crispy cabbage is one example. Once you catch a northern or two from such a weed bed, look it over carefully. How thick is it? What is the surrounding terrain like? How were the fish using it? Then seek out other weed beds similar in thickness and terrain on that lake and see if they, too, are fish attractors. Just as Fred knows what pockets will produce bass, you should be able to tell what weed beds will hold northerns. This means paying attention to what you are doing and analyzing those conditions that produce fish. The more familiar you are with the different locational patterns of the game fish you are seeking, the more versatile and successful you will be.

There is an old man named Gramps Peterson who appears every spring near an inlet on a lake near Brainerd, Minnesota. About the time that the first loons begin to dot the water, Gramps unfolds a lawn chair and rigs his rod with a red and white feathered jig. He casts for a few hours and, when he gets tired of standing, he rigs up a sucker minnow and a bobber and sits in his chair still-fishing. He always catches northerns. As the spring wears on, he changes his position near the inlet slightly, and about three weeks after the season opens, Gramps is gone. He's hardly a versatile angler, but he sure has that spring pattern figured out, and there's little doubt in his mind that he's going to catch fish. When the fall winds begin to blow, Gramps returns. This time he's on the opposite side of the inlet, and once again he's catching northerns—nice ones that weigh up to ten pounds.

The ability to visualize how a point like this one extends out under the water is crucial to confident angling.

Over the years so much has been said about the role of luck in fishing, that even serious-minded anglers believe in it. If you catch fish in a certain spot, it is because that spot is somehow different from the surrounding area; it is not because of luck.

Ask a "lucky" angler what he did to catch his fish, and he will immediately show you the lure that did it. But ask him what depth he was fishing and what the bottom conditions were like, and you'll most likely get a blank stare. He has learned little from his experience; he has simply caught some fish and gone on his way. But ask the same questions of a skilled angler, and he will almost paint you a picture of the fish location and bottom conditions. As he describes those conditions, you will think he was down there with a mask and flippers. What he was doing was paying attention to how his lure was working. A good jig fisherman can read weed types and bottom conditions just by the way the jig scrapes over the bottom. All the time he was catching those fish, he was visualizing where they were holding. By visualizing the conditions, you will be better able to present your lure or bait to the fish, and in doing so improve your success ratio considerably. You will also come to realize that those locational patterns will probably hold under similar circumstances on similar lakes. A story from a tournament Al fished two years ago really brings this point home.

"I was fishing a North Star Bass tournament on Lyda Lake in central Minnesota. During the two days of practice before the start of the tournament, I located a few schools of bass in the bullrushes. This is a locational pattern that I was familiar with on lakes similar to Lyda, where bass often move into areas of rushes and shallow water to feed. The wind plays a key role in determining how and when they will follow this pattern.

"On the first day of the tournament the pattern held, and I was near the top of the standings with most of my bass coming out of the rushes. By now I had the bass so well timed that I could predict that each day, as long as the weather held, they would move into the rushes about half an hour later than the day before. Soon many of the other anglers heard about my success, and on the final day of the tournament just about everyone was fishing the bullrushes during the early morning hours. The weather was about the same except that the wind had changed direction, and none of us did very well. By afternoon, almost everyone had left the shallows and was fishing the drop-offs and deeper water—everyone, that is, except me and my partner.

"We were still in the rushes, and we kept coming back to one section, an area that had drawn a complete blank the day before. Because of the change in the wind, I just knew that sooner or later the bass were going to be there. After the fourth trip back, my partner started getting nervous. We had gone four hours without a strike. He began suggesting that we leave the shallows and begin fishing deeper, but I was stubborn. Once more we headed back to the rushes, and once more we had no luck. Finally, on the sixth trip, we struck gold. The bass had moved in and were stacked up like cordwood. In the next twenty minutes I caught enough bass to win the tournament. My confidence in fishing the rushes combined with some good old perseverance finally paid off."

JUST ONE MORE CAST

How many times have you caught a fish on the last cast of the day? Or, on the other hand, how many times have you caught a fish on the very first cast? If you are like most of us, your percentage on those two casts is much higher than the other two or three hundred casts you make in a full day of fishing. Why? Anticipation is part of the answer, and anticipation is a big part of confidence. Usually we are really keyed up for fishing on that first cast, and we expect

to catch a fish. Because we expect a fish, we pay close attention to what we are doing. Our concentration is keen, and
our body is tensed like a spring trap, just waiting to be
triggered. If a fish strikes, we are more than ready. The
same is true of the last cast. We redouble our efforts for
that final cast, hoping against hope that a lunker will grab
our lure.

All good tournament anglers fish the entire day the way
you do on your first and last cast. They believe that every
cast is in view of a fish, and they do everything they can to
make that lure look enticing to the fish.

In a recent tournament in Florida most of us were having
terrible luck. With a combination of bad weather conditions and cold, murky water, the bass were tough to come
by. By the last day of the tournament, some of the biggest
names in fishing were way down in the listings, and Bill
Dance, one of the top bass pros around, was among them.
Bill knew that he couldn't take first place, but he never
quit trying. He worked his crank baits with all the finesse he
had, convinced that something had to break. Finally, with
only fifteen minutes left in the final day of the tournament,
he headed in. On the way to the dock he stopped near a
weedy point for just one more try. On three casts he landed
three big bass that boosted him from fortieth position all
the way to sixth place. He just refused to give up. His combination of perseverance, anticipation, and positive attitude
made the difference and, even though he didn't win, he
proved that a confident angler is never out of the running.

You don't have to be a tournament pro, however, to be
confident, nor do you have to be extremely versatile. Some
days even the best of us don't catch fish, but when this
happens, a confident angler will learn something that is
going to improve his fishing the next time out. Stay with it.
Every time out should be a learning experience, and if you
have a positive attitude, it will be.

chapter 10

When Fishing Used to Be Fun

Not many anglers have a trophy carp mounted on their wall, but Dan Gapen does. Dan is one of the Midwest's foremost river fishermen, and he has fished for exotic tucunare bass in South America and for trophy char in the upper reaches of the North American continent. So why hang a twenty-two pound carp on your wall when all these other trophies are available? Well, one reason for the appearance of Old Puckerpuss, as Dan affectionately calls him, is to make a point about the sport of fishing.

Long ago, certain sportsmen began to classify fish according to their fighting ability and according to their desirability as table fare. Thus we have the standard breakdown of game fish, panfish, and rough fish. Game fish, supposedly, are the best eating and the best fighters. Panfish are good to eat but not much sport on rod and reel. And at the bottom of the barrel are the poor rough fish, esteemed neither as food nor for their fighting ability.

The only problem with this classification system is that it is arbitrary. "Beauty is in the eye of the beholder," after all, and it seems unfair to tell anglers which fish they should pursue or ignore. Even the experts don't agree. French

Dan Gapen with his trophy carp.

chefs, the best in the world, list the catfish ahead of the walleye as an eating fish, and anyone who has caught both species would have to give the catfish the fighting edge. Yet in our country the walleye is one of the most sought-after game fish, and many of us look down our noses at catfish. In Europe, and particularly in England, the carp is well respected as a game fish, second only to trout, but in the United States it is scorned.

Generations of anglers might have really enjoyed fishing for a wider variety of fish if they hadn't dumped some of them into the rough fish category. It's obvious that some fish are not too tasty when pan fried, but often this is not the fault of the fish. Many fish are excellent when smoked and, with a little imagination, almost any fish can be made palatable. But let's assume that some fish are beyond culinary redemption. So what? What they lack in taste, they often make up for in fighting ability.

The point of all this is that perhaps we need to rethink what fishing is all about. Chet Meyers still remembers the first time he and Al Lindner met, and his story illustrates that even professional anglers still retain that childlike joy of catching panfish.

"I met Al for the first time in Brainerd, Minnesota, about three years ago. I had an appointment to talk with him about a fishing school at which he was going to serve as the main speaker. I arrived at his office a little early and was told that he was out fishing on his lunch break. It was the middle of April, and I couldn't help but wonder what he was fishing for when most of the ground was still covered with snow. In a few minutes Al came trudging in with his hip boots and winter jacket. He wore a huge grin, and I could tell that he had done well. After introductions I asked,

" 'What the heck were you fishing for? Walleye season doesn't open for another four weeks.'

" 'Crappie.'

" 'You mean the famous Al Lindner still fishes for crappies?'

"Al then proceeded to tell me about a school of crappies he had located in the Mississippi River, less than two hundred yards from his office. By the end of his discourse, I was ready to forget all about our meeting and head for the river. I knew from that moment that here was a real sportsman—he really loved fishing. And crappies were just as good as walleyes in his mind."

It's sad that some anglers feel it beneath them to fish for anything other than a few select species of fish. We recently ran into such an individual while fishing a lake that had a good population of largemouth bass and northerns. It was early in the fall and, after catching a few bass, we decided to switch tactics and see if the northerns had begun their fall migration into shallower water. There was only one other boat on the lake, and from the way the two occupants were working over a submerged weedbed, it looked as if they knew what they were doing. As we pulled near them, we asked if they had caught any northerns. It was like setting off a charge of dynamite. One angler told us straight off that he wasn't going to fish for those "slimy snakes." He then proceeded to slander the northern as if it were his bitterest enemy. Not only did they smell, he said, but they also chewed up all his best lures. We listened for a few minutes and then slowly motored away.

Judging from all the equipment in his boat and from the award patches on his bass jacket, the man was probably a good bass angler. If he is so prejudiced against northerns, one can only wonder what he thinks of carp. Of course, each of us has the right to fish for whatever he prefers. But before we write off any fish for its fighting and eating qualities, or simply for the pure fun of catching it, we should at least give it a fair chance. Dan Gapen is one of a new breed of anglers who treat all fish as equals. He enjoys catching just about anything that swims and returns most of his catch to the water alive. Old Puckerpuss isn't hanging on Dan's wall just to make a point. Dan honestly enjoys fishing for carp, and so will increasing numbers of anglers once they give it a try.

FISHING AS A SERIOUS BUSINESS

Not long ago most of us went fishing simply to relax and get away from the pressures of daily life. With a can of worms, rod and reel, and a ragged assortment of lures and hooks, we took off for our favorite lake or river. Though we always hoped for a stringer of lunkers, we knew the odds were pretty much against us and were reasonably satisfied with whatever fish came our way. Just being out of doors and relaxing on the water was enough reward in itself. For many people fishing still has this therapeutic value, but for increasing numbers fishing has become a serious business.

We are not talking necessarily about professional fishermen, because the best of the pros still experience the pure joy of fishing and accept poor fishing days along with the good ones. There are, however, a growing number of weekend anglers who feel they have to bring in their limit each time out, just to prove to the world they are truly competent anglers. If they fail to produce, they are tired and defeated. Instead of enjoying a weekend away from work, they need to get back to work in order to relax. What's happened to make this once enjoyable sport such a serious business for so many people?

Perhaps the biggest reason for this change in attitudes is that our level of expectations has been raised. Back in the "good old days" we were willing to take what nature had to offer, and we didn't expect to come in with a quantity of fish after each outing. But with the advent of modern electronic fishing equipment such as depth finders, oxygen meters, temperature gauges and the like, we began to believe that success was guaranteed. Rather than accepting our losses as inevitable, we came to feel that we should win each time out, and so far as the sport of fishing is concerned, this attitude is downright unrealistic.

When properly used, modern equipment can improve the odds, and increasing our versatility as anglers will certainly bring in more fish, but all of us are going to get "skunked" sometimes, and the poor fishing days are bound to outnumber the good ones. Even the pros get skunked. At a recent bass tournament in northern Minnesota, more than half the contestants didn't land a bass in two days of fishing, and last year's winner of a southern tournament had only one fourteen-inch bass to his credit. Buck Perry, the dean of structure fishing, said it best. "Fishing is usually bad, and most often it gets worse." Rather than competing

Even the best equipment in the hands of an expert does not spell success every time out.

with nature, perhaps we need to lower our expectations a little so that we can begin to enjoy the other benefits that fishing has to offer—relief from the tensions of life, the companionship of a friend, and the beauty of the natural world.

Let's pretend for a moment that it is evening on a small bass pond in your part of the country. You've eaten an early dinner so that you can spend three or four hours wading the edge of this pond in search of lunker bass. You have the entire pond to yourself, and it's so silent that you almost feel like a trespasser. A muskrat glides silently by, not even aware of your presence. You are alone. There is no pressure to produce since no one will know if you catch anything or not. You could even sit back and watch the sun go down without wetting a line. But suddenly you see a swirl on the surface of the water where a fish made a pass at some minnows. Then you see another boil and some minnows skipping across the surface, desperately trying to escape their underwater pursuer. Your body tenses with excitement. You tie on your favorite surface lure and cast it out on the now calm surface.

Nothing happens.

You make a few twitches and slowly begin the retrieve. You pause. Your heart is pounding a little in anticipation. At any second you expect to see the waters part and the bass inhale your lure. Eventually, after a few more casts, you begin to relax again. Maybe that swirl was just a snapping turtle, and maybe those minnows were just jumping for joy.

Once again the silence of the evening drifts over you. You begin to look around. Where did that muskrat go? A bullfrog begins its nightly serenade and a little green heron begins stalking the shallows for minnows. You watch the bird slowly wade along; at times it is completely motionless before the sudden lunge that assures it a meal. Soon you no

Sometimes there is more to fishing than catching fish.

longer feel like an intruder. This is fishing for pure relaxation. You came seeking bass, but you have cast for over three hours without a strike, and now you don't even care. As the Bible says, there is a time for all things. Tonight was a time for fishing; some other day will be the time for catching.

MOMENTS TO REMEMBER

Perhaps one of the most enjoyable things about angling is the unanticipated surprise that it often provides us. There are times when we start out with the goal of catching some lunkers and end up watching the sun go down. There are other times when we go out just to relax, with no hope of catching anything bigger than a few crappies or eating-size walleyes, and our efforts are rewarded with an unexpected bonus. Al Lindner had such an experience in October of 1976.

"Late that fall for about three weeks, we had exceptionally low water on the Mississippi River near my home. Severe drought conditions had dropped the river to an all-time low, and in many places it was difficult even to get a boat in the water. Except for a few anglers who were willing to wade the river, there was little fishing pressure. Most of the fish were concentrated in the deepest pools. Since walleyes in the river below the Brainerd Dam were stacked like cordwood, we were releasing all the fish we caught. Two men fishing two or three hours a night could catch thirty to fifty walleyes in the 1½- to 2-pound category without any problem.

"When Mort Bank from Bismarck, North Dakota, and Bill Olmsted, my insurance agent, paid a visit, I suggested we hit the river after the working day was finished for a couple of hours of fun fishing. I knew that walleyes were there, but I wasn't prepared for the surprise that awaited us. We put in below the dam and had a triple header on before we had moved more than a few yards. In forty-five minutes we went through six dozen minnows! Initially, we were fishing with jigs tipped with minnows or with minnows on live bait rigs. When we ran out of minnows, I figured that the action was so fast that the walleyes would take a plain jig, so I switched to a black jig and continued to take fish.

"We moved around the pool little by little and finally

decided to anchor in between two points in a trough that was about twelve feet deep. In this position we were within casting distance of both points. It was just bing, bing, bing —a fish on almost every cast. The ¼-ounce jig would hit bottom, and a walleye would grab it. If you missed one, you just dropped the jig back down, and another one would grab it. As it began to get dark, we moved back to the other side of the pool. We pulled in front of a paper mill discharge tube that feeds water back into the river. This warmer 'processed' water can sometimes really pull in the fish. It wasn't long before Mort set the hook into something big. At first he thought it was a snag, but after a jerk of the rod the line began slowly moving up river. Puzzled by the lack of fight, Mort said, 'This fish acts like it isn't even hooked or aggravated. I don't think it knows it's hooked.'

This current breakline between the warm water discharge of the power plant and the river current is where Mort's battle with the monster began.

©**In' Fisherman** magazine

"I thought Mort had snagged a big buffalo or red horse sucker. He started back reeling the fish and exerted little tension since he was using only six-pound test. The fish continued to run upriver, and it was obvious that Mort wasn't going to turn it. I didn't want to move from our spot because all the time Mort was fighting his fish, Bill and I were still catching walleyes. 'Break the line,' I told him. 'You've snagged into a buffalo.' 'Let me get a look at this fish,' Mort answered. 'It may be a buffalo, but it's got to be a thirty-pounder. I want to play with it for a while.' So I lifted the anchor and started to follow the fish.

"Mort had hooked that fish at about five o'clock, forty-five minutes before dark. It was now five-thirty. All this time the fish was seemingly unaware that it was even hooked. Finally, the fish made one good run, a real burst of speed that just peeled off the line. I knew then that it wasn't a buffalo. As the line started to come up, out in the hazy distance I saw the tail break the surface. From the looks of it, Mort had hooked a huge northern, and now I began to get serious. Bill and I had been casting and picking up walleyes while Mort had been playing his monster. We pulled in our lines and concentrated on following that fish. After the initial run, the fish worked us into some really fast water that was shooting out of the side of the dam. As it hit the fast water, it broke water for the first time, about twenty-five feet from the boat, and we had our first good look at the mystery monster. It was a muskie and a big one! Mort was in a state of shock, and I was getting really nervous.

" 'It's dark,' I thought. 'We've been fighting this fish for over an hour, and Mort's line is frayed. There are snags in the river. With all those log jams the fish is bound to get wrapped up.' Then I looked in the boat and, to my disbelief, found that we didn't have a large net, a gaff, or even a club. There wasn't a single thing to help us land the fish. I asked some bank fishermen if they had a net, and all they had to offer was a trout net that might have fit over the fish's head. It was time to make some quick decisions. I told Mort to ease off on the fish while I pulled close to shore and dropped Bill off. Bill drove into downtown Brainerd to a tackle store and bought the biggest net available. Meanwhile, the fish was swimming all over the pool, and several times it came within a few feet of the boat.

"It was now one hour and fifteen minutes since Mort first hooked the fish. The next time it approached the boat, we saw that it was only slightly hooked in the lip. Time was against us, and in favor of the fish. I wanted to take a chance and grab it. I figured I would just lay my hands underneath and, in one quick sweep, try to flop it in the boat. I had done this before in my guiding days, but never with such a huge fish. It looked as if it might weigh forty pounds. Incredibly, the fish was alongside the boat, looking straight at us. It seemed really beat, but then you never know. Suddenly, with a last surge of energy, it took off and ran all the way back to where we first hooked it. Then it simply bulldogged down to the bottom and stayed there. Now we had no choice except to wait until the net arrived.

"When Bill returned with the net, we had crossed the river, and he was on the wrong side. So there we sat—net on one side of the river and muskie on the other. Bill saw the situation immediately and drove back down to the bridge, across the river, and up to the paper mill. He spent a few agonizing moments trying to convince a gate guard at the mill that there were two guys down on the river with a monster fish hooked that needed a landing net. The guard looked at Bill and said, 'Sure, buddy!' Finally, Bill convinced the guard to let him through and arrived with the net and a flashlight in hand.

"Mort back reeled, leaving the fish in the pool, while I pulled us into shore. Bill climbed aboard, and I maneuvered the boat out to where our monster lay waiting. Slowly Mort

Al, Mort, and Bill with a "keeper" muskie—and all they were after was a few walleyes.

©In' Fisherman magazine

began to exert pressure, and the muskie responded. Unfortunately, it had had time to regain its strength, and it took off for an area that was filled with log jams. I was sure we were going to lose it, but Mort really came through. He managed to turn the fish and head it in toward the boat. I felt as if I were about to net a small submarine. As the muskie came to the boat, I placed the net underneath it and, to prevent the net from breaking, grabbed the metal loop and lifted the fish into the boat. And was it a fish—forty-four pounds, one ounce, and fifty-four inches long!

"To think that twice I had told Mort to break the fish off because I figured he had hooked a buffalo. Can you imagine that? Boy, did I learn a lesson! That fish was the second biggest muskie to come out of Minnesota that year. And all because one guy refused to give up on a buffalo."

chapter 11

Learning
to Let Go

While we have come a long way towards understanding fish
and the sport of fishing, there is still much mystery. Fish
are ancient animals, which have inhabited our earthly environment much longer than we humans have. Their reasoning powers are almost nonexistent when compared with
ours, but their instinct for survival is strong. Every day
there are subtle changes in weather and water conditions of
which we are unaware, but which fish recognize and react
to instinctively. And though we have begun to understand
the basics of fish movement, there are some aspects of their
behavior that we may never fully comprehend. There will
still be those days when all our knowledge and skills fail,
and we return to the dock "skunked," confounded by these
creatures of little brain. Perhaps this is good. Certainly part
of the attraction of fishing is coping with the unexpected.

In the final analysis, the sport of fishing will always re-
quire playing the percentages. The complexities of nature
assure that we will never be able to predict exactly how
fish will behave under a given circumstance. But even
though our understanding of fish behavior is limited, our
control over their environment is tremendous.

Anglers can no longer take for granted an unlimited supply of clean water teeming with fish. Pollution has taken its toll of our water resources, and there is the old problem of supply and demand as well. Each year there are more anglers and fewer fish to go around. Anyone who has spent opening day on some of our more crowded lakes and rivers knows what intense fishing pressure is like. It is time for anglers to step forward as advocates for the preservation of quality fishing. We need to inform our state legislatures and local governments of our interest in the protection of waters from industrial and agricultural pollution. Moreover, each of us can play a role in the maintenance of quality fishing by sharing the fish that are available with others.

Fishing is much like the sport of hunting. There is the thrill of the pursuit, the pride in the trophy, and the therapy of being close to nature. Angling differs, however, in one very important aspect: The trophy can be released to swim and fight again. It might seem strange to end a book on fishing by suggesting that, after all the time and energy we spend to catch fish, we should turn around and release them. But when you consider that the increasing number of knowledgeable anglers adds to the already heavy fishing pressure on lakes and rivers, it is obvious that we are going to have to do something if we want to continue to enjoy quality fishing. Releasing part of one's catch is a new ethic among anglers, and there is much to be said in its favor.

A group of muskie addicts called Muskies Incorporated was one of the first to promote this ethic. Because of its habits and habitat needs, the muskie will never be able to populate lakes in large numbers. In addition to stocking muskies in likely waters, Muskies Incorporated provided an incentive for its member to release legal size muskies by awarding colorful embroidered "release patches" for their fishing jackets. Their program is a great success. Some

There is a lot of satisfaction in releasing your fish so that others can enjoy it someday.

of the proudest anglers we know are not ones with trophies hanging on the wall, but those with release patches sewn on their jackets.

A similar policy is put into practice in many of the bass tournaments held across the country each year. Tournament boats are equipped with live wells, which are small holding tanks with circulating water, so that the fish can be kept alive until weigh-in time at the end of the day. Anglers receive additional points for every live bass they bring in. Then, at day's end, all the bass are put into a giant holding tank and kept overnight to make sure they are healthy. The next day they are released back into the lake. Tournament officials estimate that close to 90 percent of the bass taken in this way live to fight again. For those of us who don't fish tournaments, an even better way to ensure healthy released fish is to let them go as quickly as possible.

TIPS ON RELEASING YOUR CATCH

Fish are very fragile when they are out of the water. Those that are caught uninjured, minimally handled, and released quickly, however, have an excellent chance of surviving. Here are a few suggestions that will ensure that the fish you release will survive.

- If there is no legal size limit, keep any fish that is bleeding from the gill area. The gills of a fish are the most fragile and vulnerable of organs, and any injury to them that results in bleeding means almost certain death to the fish. Here common sense sometimes runs counter to the law, for many states have size limits that prohibit keeping small fish. If your state has no such law, then keep small injured fish. You may feel strange keeping a twelve-inch walleye, but returning it to the lake is just wasting game.

- If you intend to release a fish, bring it to the net quickly. The longer you force a fish to fight, the more lactic acid builds up in the fish's muscle system. A fish that is completely exhausted from battle may have enough energy to swim away from your boat only to die a few hours later. Trout are particularly susceptible to this type of death since lactic acid buildup may not peak until one or two hours after the initial exertion.

- If you have landed a fish and want to release it, try to keep it in the water while removing the hooks. Lifting a fish out of the water is a severe shock to the fish's internal organs, which seldom feel the full effect of the earth's gravity. If you must remove the fish from the water, moisten your hand to prevent removal of the protective layer of slime, and lay the fish on its side. Do not hold the fish by its head because the internal organs are then hanging in an unnatural position.

- If you are going to release a northern pike, do not grab it by the eye sockets. The eye-hold tactic is often recommended because it paralyzes the fish and facilitates lure removal. The problem is that this hold can permanently blind the fish. Because northerns are primarily sight feeders, blindness results in a slow, painful death. Use a wet burlap sack and grasp the fish firmly behind the gill covers.

- If a fish is "gut hooked," as often happens when fishing with live bait, cut off the line as close as possible to the hook and let it remain. Since fish have extremely strong acid in their digestive tracks, the hook will begin to dissolve within a few days. If you pull on the hook and distend the fish's intestines, you may do irreparable damage.

By suggesting this new approach to angling, we do not mean to sentimentalize the sport or to suggest that all fish should be released. We often fish not only for the catching, but also for the eating. There are times, however, when we bring home too many fish for our needs or just to impress our family and neighbors with the size and number of our catch. A photograph of the fish before it is released serves the latter purpose just as well as the fish on the stringer. And as far as fish dinners are concerned, the smaller fish are usually better eating. Why not release some of the larger ones so that someone else can enjoy catching them?

Learning to release some of your catch without harming the fish will not only help to provide better fishing for others, it will also give you a sense of self-satisfaction and a renewed respect for the creatures you pursue. If you are after a trophy for your wall, set a weight limit for yourself and throw back the fish that don't meet your goal. It's a good feeling to know that a bass or walleye that provided a few moments of excitement and pleasure is back there in the depths, swimming free.

Appendix

This brief appendix is prepared to assist the beginning angler in the selection of proper fishing tackle. We have intentionally focused on freshwater spinning, spin-casting, and bait-casting equipment. Our suggestions for quality equipment are based on personal use and preference. There are many manufacturers who market fishing tackle of fine quality, and in general, the angler can be guided by purchasing name brand items.

RODS AND REELS

Fishing rods and reels must be considered together, since a good reel matched to the proper rod are the basic tools of successful angling. The concept of matched equipment simply means that you have the right size reel on the right action rod and use them under the right conditions.

A few years ago, an angler looking for equipment wandered into the local tackle store and chose a rod and reel from the rather meager selection on the store rack. Today, however, many sporting goods stores have hundreds of rods and reels from which to choose. While some of them are designed to meet the weekend angler's general fishing needs, each year we see more and more specialty equipment. There are "worming rods" for bass addicts, speed-trolling rods for northern pike enthusiasts, ultralight rods for trout and panfish anglers, and recently, a confusing array of graphite rods. Reels are not quite as complicated, but there is still a wide variety available.

So where do you start in selecting the tackle that will meet your particular needs? The choice of the best rod and reel for your purposes becomes less of a mystery if you take time to answer a few simple questions before you go shopping.

- How often do you go fishing? If you fish only a few weekends out of the year and want an outfit that can meet the general fishing needs for most panfish and game fish, then you can probably get by with one or two inexpensive rods and reels. There are a number of moderately priced good quality rods and reels to choose from and, given the limited amount of action that this equipment will see, it makes little sense to spend a lot of money. Beware, however, of cut-rate packaged outfits that seem irresistible because of the low price tag. You should be prepared to spend about twenty-five dollars for a good reel and somewhat less for a stable rod.

- What type of fish will you be fishing for most often? Muskie and northern pike anglers need stiff rods with lots of backbone to set the hooks into bony mouths. The panfish enthusiast, however, should use a limber rod and light line when seeking the tender-mouthed crappie. If you want to be prepared for a variety of different types of fishing, then select a rod with medium action, a flexible tip, and enough backbone so that you can handle a real lunker when you tie into one.

- What types of lakes will you usually be fishing, and what will your tactics be? Ultralight spinning tackle is suitable when fishing for smallmouth bass in clear, weed-free Canadian lakes, but southern anglers who are after bass in timber and heavy weeds usually go with a bait-casting outfit and fifteen- to twenty-pound test line. If you spend most of your time casting, you will want a rod with a flexible tip so you won't wear out your arm. If you like to back troll for walleyes, on the other hand, then your rod should have a fairly stiff tip and should be one piece so that it can transmit the sensitive "take" when a walleye sucks up your worm or minnow.

Most tackle stores have trained personnel who can direct you to the proper equipment once you tell them what you are after. After you actually start looking at the different models, keep the following considerations in mind.

Rod Selection

- Make sure the ferrules, where the rod sections join together, are snug fitting and the windings around the guides are tight.

- The normal chrome guides on most rods are not long lasting. If you spend lots of time casting, then ask for a rod with carboloy guides or the new ceramic ones made of aluminum oxide.

- Avoid "buggy whip" rods that shake and shimmy from the tip to the butt. Make sure that your rod has sufficient backbone to handle large fish.

- Check the reel seating device to make sure that your reel will fit. Don't assume that all reels fit all rods—they don't. Either take your own reel along or ask the salesperson for one of the store's.

Reel Selection

• If you have only enough for either a good reel or a good rod, put your money into the reel. A quality reel will outlast many rods, and a good medium spinning reel can be used on a number of different rods.

• Make sure that your reel has easily interchangeable spools. Purchase at least one additional spool so you can change from ten-pound test to six-pound test when the conditions call for it.

• Avoid gimmicky rod and reel combinations in which the reel is permanently affixed to the rod.

• Ask the salesperson if the reel is easily repaired and check the instruction book. Spinning-reel bail springs break often, and you should be able to make such minor repairs in the boat.

While there are many ways to classify rods and reels, we have come up with the system shown in the chart opposite, which focuses on the particular species that the angler chooses to pursue.

A Word About Graphite Rods

Each year the equipment industry puts some new piece of "wonder" equipment on the market, and in recent years graphite rods are in the spotlight. These rods come in all sizes to fit any of the aforementioned purposes. They are more expensive than most fiberglass rods, but they will probably get cheaper as competition drives the price down. Graphite rods are much lighter than glass rods and are extremely strong. They are also very sensitive, and you can feel every turn of a spinner blade when working them. If you decide to purchase a graphite rod, remember that in spite of their strength, they can break very easily with even

CATEGORY	ROD MANUFACTURER AND MODEL NUMBER	REEL MANUFACTURER AND MODEL NUMBER
Ultralight spinning (Trout, panfish, and bass)	Fenwick 952 Skyline SKC 5504	Zebco Cardinal 3 Shakespeare 2400
General purpose spinning (Walleyes, bass, and small northerns)	Lew Childre 4-266HSML Fenwick PLS64	Garcia Mitchell 300A Quick 220
General purpose spin casting (Walleyes, bass, and small northerns)	Heddon 5007 Berkley B10	Garcia 170 Johnson 140C
Casting (Bass in weeds and timber)	Skyline CSK 558 Fenwick 2061	Garcia Ambassadeur 4500C Shakespeare President II 1980
Heavy duty casting (Muskies and northerns)	Skyline Muskie Special Fenwick 2057	Garcia Ambassadeur 6500C Shakespeare President 1981
Specialty Rods and Reels Back trolling	Skyline 6007 Lew Childre 1-266HSML	Zebco Cardinal 4 Shakespeare 2410
Speed trolling	Spoon Plugger* Pro Fisherman Formula 4**	Penn 109 Compac 1000
Worming (plastic worms)	Skyline CSK 559	Garcia Ambassadeur 5500C

* Not marketed nationally. Contact Buck Perry, P.O. Box 444, Mt. Juliet, TN 37122
** Not marketed nationally. Contact Chuck Hamer, Profisherman Manufacturers, 2655 Midvale Place, St. Paul, MN 55119

Recommended rod and reel combinations.

the slightest nick. Keep them in a carrying case at all times when not in use and treat them as you would any fine tool.

FISHING LINE

Fishing line, particularly monofilament line, is probably the least considered and yet most important part of one's fishing equipment. Anglers will spend hundreds of dollars on rods and reels, and then try to skimp by purchasing one thousand yards of line for sixty-nine cents. If the truth were known, more lunkers are lost to cheap or poorly cared for line than for any other reason.

- Buy name brand line of high quality. Remember, your line is the only thing between you and the fish. If you want to save money, go together with a few friends and purchase good quality line in bulk.

- Constantly check your rod guides and your reel for potential rough spots. When you can see cracks or frays in your line, it usually means that your guides are worn and need to be changed.

- Change your line every year. Most monofilament has a shelf life of less than two years. This means that the strength of the line decreases in time even in storage. Make sure that the line you purchase is newly manufactured. Stores sometimes have clearance sales and unload line that is two or three years old.

- Direct sunlight destroys the molecular structure of monofilament. When not in use, store your reel in a cool, dry, dark spot. Do not leave your rod in the back of a locked car where sunlight and heat can weaken the line.

We recommend the following quality brand lines.

- *Monofilament spinning, spin casting, and bait casting:* Dupont Stren, Berkley Trilene, and Garcia Bonnyl.

- *Monofilament speed trolling line:* No-Bo

- *Braided nylon casting line:* Cortland and Gudebrod

DEPTH FINDERS

One of the questions most often asked by individuals who are just getting started in fishing is, "Do I have to buy a depth finder to be a successful angler?" Naturally, the answer depends on the type of fishing that one most enjoys. A fly fisherman on the clear, shallow trout streams of Colorado has little need for a depth finder. Similarly, a farm pond fisherman back East, who spends most of his time on ponds less than ten acres in size, can discover the depth range by making a few casts with a deep-diving lure. An angler fishing a five-thousand-acre walleye lake in northern Minnesota, however, is going to waste a lot of time and miss valuable fish-holding structure unless he has a depth finder.

On larger bodies of water, a quality depth finder used with a contour map is going to increase one's fishing success immeasureably. The map gives the angler some idea of the general lake contours, and the depth finder helps to locate fishing "hot spots" that seldom show up on maps. Learning to use a depth finder is a real art, and those who are considering purchasing one should spend some time with a friend who owns one and can demonstrate its pros and cons.

While there are over thirty different manufacturers and over one hundred models on the market, there are three basic types of units that anglers should be aware of.

- *Flasher units:* These units indicate depths on a circular dial by using a sonar unit and a high-speed rotating light bulb. The depth dials vary in range. Most freshwater fishermen in inland lakes and rivers do very well with a sixty-foot range. Anglers on the Great Lakes will probably want readings that go over one hundred feet. If you do have a unit with only a sixty-foot dial, the depth finder will record greater depths by making one complete revolution of the dial and then starting over. Thus, on a unit with a sixty-foot range, a fifteen-foot reading in deep water indicates an actual depth of seventy-five feet.

- *Graphing units:* These units record depths and illustrate bottom contours on graph paper. They are generally much more expensive than the flasher units. When they first came out, the graph units created quite a stir because they actually show fish and can distinguish between schools of bait fish and large game fish. To many anglers this sounded like the magic solution they had been looking for. Well, it isn't! The mere presence of fish does not guarantee success, since fish are in a neutral or negative feeding mood 90 percent of the time. A friend of ours once spent the good part of a day fishing over a school of walleyes that showed up on his graph. The fish were not feeding, but he was so fascinated by seeing them on the graph and knowing that they were under his boat that he couldn't tear himself away. Meanwhile, anglers on other parts of the lake were catching feeding walleyes.

  One limitation of these units is that the bottom contours are distorted when the boat is run at a fast speed. For the beginning angler a graphing unit is probably not the best investment.

- *Combination graph and flasher units:* These units have both a flasher dial and a separate graphing printout. They are expensive and should not be considered a necessary investment for the novice angler.

Getting the Most Out of Your Flasher Unit

Although depth finders were originally advertised as fish locators, they are used primarily to determine water depth and to locate underwater structure. A good depth finder, however, can tell you even more than this. With a little practice on the water you can learn not only how to locate structure, but also how to determine the bottom content, the presence of weeds and sunken timber, and the presence of fish.

All depth finders operate on the principle of sonar. Electrical impulses are transmitted to the bottom and are recorded as they bounce back to the sending and receiving unit. These impulses show up as a light band on the circular dial. The presence of a hard gravel or mud bottom shows up as a sharp, narrow band on the depth dial. Softer bottoms that absorb some of these impulses usually register as a wide, rather weak band. Since fish most often avoid soft mucky bottoms, a good depth finder can help you eliminate unproductive areas of a lake. Weeds show up as small light flashes originating at the bottom and light up a band on the dial according to their height. Brush and timber often give a similar reading though large trees trigger a stronger signal. Fish show up as intermittent flashes as they pass quickly through the signal.

As with any tool, a certain amount of care is necessary for a depth finder unit to perform consistently. There are two primary parts of these units: (1) the main component box and reading dial or graph, and (2) the transducer, which sends out and receives the signals. The main cause of damage to depth finders is due to acid leakage from batteries. Batteries should be removed from the main component box and the entire unit wiped dry after use. The condensation from water can weaken transformers and other component units. On the Hummingbird unit recommended below, the entire main component is waterproof, and drying is not necessary.

After purchasing a depth finder, it is crucial to mount the transducer properly so that it reads straight down and is in constant contact with the water while the boat is running. The mounting system of many units is a cheap rubber suction cup attached to the back of the transom. Such cups often twist or pull off, giving an incorrect depth reading. We would recommend that you either purchase an exterior transducer bracket that screws to the back of your boat's transom or, if you do all your fishing from one boat, consider having the transducer permanently mounted through the hull or in the boat bottom.

Choosing the Depth Finder Best for You

There is no way to fully assess a depth finder's quality in the store. While various "in store" tests have been devised, the only way to check out a unit thoroughly is on the water. For this reason we suggest that you find a friend who can demonstrate a particular unit and then talk with other anglers about the pros and cons of their units. We personally recommend the following units for consistency of quality and long life.

- *Flasher units:* Hummingbird Super Sixty, Lowrance LFP-300D, and Heathkits, which are ready-to-assemble kits for do-it-yourselfers.

- *Graphing unit:* Vexilar 555

- *Combination graph and flasher:* Lowrance 605A

Index

anchoring in wind, 68
back trolling, 67-68, 134-136, 143
barometric pressure, 70-73
bass, plastic worms for, 126; predictability of movement in, 13; rain and, 70; shad as food source of, 81; spawning of, 36; weeds and, 47; winter dormancy of, 12. *See also* largemouth bass; smallmouth bass
Binkleman, Bill, 132, 137-138
bottom conditions, 32, 35-36, 44, 85, 160
bulrushes, 39
cabbage, 36, 40, *41, 42,* 46-47, 48
cabomba, 40, *41, 42,* 47
carp, 163, 164
catfish, 164
cattails, 35, 38, *39*
cloud cover, 54
cold front, 55-58
coontail, 40, *41, 42,* 47
cork jigs, 137-138
crank baits, 111-112
curly cabbage, *41*
daily log, 14, *16,* 17-18, 32, 33
daily movements of fish, 17-21. *See also* weather, effect of, on fish
department of natural resources. *See* natural resources, state departments of
depth, 32, 85-86, 106-109
depth finders, 25, 29, 35, 95-96, 187-190
dressings, jig, 147
eel grass, 40, *41*
fall turnover, 12
fertility of lakes, 34-35, 80
fish, attack response of, 120-124, 144; barometric pressure and, 70-73; behavior patterns and instincts of, 28-29; bottom conditions and, 32; daily movements of, 17-21; depth and, 32; differing growth rates of, 79-82; effect of rain on, 69; "gut hooking" of, 180; light penetration and, 32; live bait and, 130-131; release of, 179-180; seasonal movements of, 8-17; spawning of, 9, 11, 14, 16, 28, 36; ultraviolet rays and, 56-57; water clarity and, 88-89; water levels and, 86-88; water temperature and, 14; weather and, 50-58; weeds and, 36-37
fishing line, 186-187
flowage lakes, 86-87
Gapen, Dan, 163, 166
gills, fragility of, 179
graphite rods, 184-185
hard bottom weeds, 39-40
hornwort, 40
hydrographic maps, 13-14, *15, 30,* 82, 84-85, 96
jig and eel combination, 48
jig and minnow combination, 46, 49, 66, 145-*150*
jigs, 114-115, 137-138
lactic acid, buildup of, 179
lakes, age and bottom conditions of, 34-35; selection of, 73-92; surveys of, 94-103; water level fluctuation in, 86-87
largemouth bass, cold front passage and, 59; lily pads and, 38; plastic worms and, 124; reeds as indicator of, 39; seasonal patterns of, 102-103; shallow water and, 44; spawning of, 85; weed beds and, 44
light penetration, fish behavior and, 32, 36-37, 54-55; measuring depth of, 89-90; water clarity and, 88; weed growth and, 90; wind and, 62. *See also* water clarity
lily pads, 32, 38, *39, 42*
Lindner, Ron, 56, 132